Affairs of State

Also by George Austin

Journey to Faith

Affairs of State

A Study in Leadership, Religion and Society

George Austin, Archdeacon of York

Hodder & Stoughton
LONDON SYDNEY AUCKLAND

To Canon Geoffrey Ainsworth Williams, who first
guided me to recognise my vocation to the priesthood

First published in Great Britain in 1995
by Hodder and Stoughton Ltd,
a division of Hodder Headline PLC

10 9 8 7 6 5 4 3 2

British Library Cataloguing in Publication Data

A record for this book is available from the British Library

ISBN 0 340 62140 0

Typeset by Hewer Text Composition Services, Edinburgh
Printed and bound in Great Britain by
Cox & Wyman, Reading, Berks

Hodder and Stoughton Ltd,
A division of Hodder Headline PLC
338 Euston Road
London NW1 3BH

Contents

Acknowledgments

Thanks are due to the following for permission to quote extracts:

Antony Jay Productions and Ally Pally Enterprises by permission of Imison Playwrights Ltd for *Yes, Prime Minister* (1986);
OUP for various books listed in the Notes;
The Church Commissioners for England and The Central Board of Finance of the Church of England for *Crockford's Clerical Directory* and *Reports of Proceedings of the General Synod* (1987);
WCC Publications, World Council of Churches, Geneva, Switzerland for Rodney Booth, *Winds of God* (1982);
A & C Black for J. R. H. Moorman, *History of the Church in England*;
SPCK for Hugh Dawes, *Freeing the Faith*;
Hamish Hamilton for William Oddie, *The Crockford Files*.

Preface

There are no easy answers to the moral complexities of our age, and this book does little more than identify the problem. But problem there is, and with it there is a growing unease at the condition of the society in which we live, together with a despair at the quality of leadership which is evident to bring us to a better world.

I write as a Christian and a traditional one at that, who believes that part of our dis-ease has its roots in the decline of spiritual values and religious commitment. If there is any kind of answer to the disorder we experience around us, then it lies fundamentally in a return to the faith once delivered to the saints.

I write too as a priest of the Church of England, who like so many fellow-Anglicans is almost in despair at the condition of the Church we love, at its ready abandonment of so many of its ideals, and at the failure of so many of its leaders to defend and support the truths and values committed to their care.

But the despair is never total: for it is God's Church and God's world and in the end he is in charge.

GEORGE AUSTIN
Feast of St Swithun, 1994

1

Introduction

There is occasions and causes why and wherefore in all things.

Henry V, v.i.3

A budding writer once asked a famous author to recommend a recipe for a successful novel and was told he must always be sure to include sex, religion and the aristocracy. So the young man sat down and typed the first sentence: 'O God,' prayed the duchess, 'please let me not be pregnant.'

This book owes its origin to sex, religion and not merely the aristocracy but the monarchy, though it is about much more than that. It all began innocently enough, with a telephone call from the independent morning television company, GMTV, at 11.45 p.m. on Monday 6 December 1993. Had I seen the report on BBC *Newsnight* that evening, and what did I think of the story in tomorrow's *Sun* newspaper which claimed that the Archbishop of Canterbury had questioned Prince Charles's suitability for the throne? No, I had not, but I was sure the denials from the Archbishop's spokesman at Lambeth were correct: it did not fit with other things he had said, and anyway the throne was occupied for the foreseeable future.

I was reluctantly persuaded to set the alarm for six the next morning, and be taken to the Yorkshire Television studios in Leeds for a live interview. Unfortunately the connection to GMTV went wrong, and I could not be heard in London. It was no one's fault, but I was not over-delighted at the unnecessary early rising. As I came back to the newsroom, someone said there was a phone-call from the BBC *Today* programme, asking for a similar interview.

Having been on the *Thought for the Day* rota for many years, I know the *Today* presenters well and hold them all in high regard. So, yes, I would talk to Peter Hobday. Were there problems for the Church of England if Charles became King? 'My view', I commented, 'would be that Charles made solemn vows in church about his marriage, and it seems – if the rumours are true about Camilla Parker-Bowles – that he began to break them almost immediately. He has broken his trust and vows to God on one thing. How can he then go into Westminster Abbey and take coronation vows? I think it brings into question the whole attitude of Charles to vows, trust and so on.'

What if he were to divorce and remarry?

I said that if this were to happen, there would be problems for some of us in the light of his role as Supreme Governor of the Church.

It was nothing I had not said before – for instance in a debate on Sky Television following a showing of an adaptation of Andrew Morton's book on the Princess of Wales, and in January 1993 in an article in the *Mail on Sunday*. Neither had produced a flicker of a reaction.

But now it was different; by the time I arrived home from the Leeds studio, the telephone had begun to ring, with requests for articles, comments and interviews. This went on without interruption until sometime after lunch when I left for a meeting in London, and judging by the fifty-four calls on the answerphone when my wife returned two days later, it had continued long afterwards.

There were those who charged me with deliberately seeking publicity, but since I was spending the whole of that week at meetings with the two archbishops, I can only say that if I were really after publicity, it was the daftest of all weeks in which to seek it. Others joked that I had suddenly 'discovered' the media, but in reality I had had a regular television slot thirty-seven years before, had written articles and had been involved in broadcasting for most of the time since then. I still enjoy it as a challenge but is not a novelty to be sought out for its own sake.

Some even accused me of trying to further my 'career', as if there should be such a thing in the Church. At the time, the General Synod had agreed that bishops be appointed to care for those opposed to the ordination of women, and my name was strongly tipped for one of these 'flying bishops' (as they came to be known popularly), but after my remarks about the heir to the throne, my name could certainly not have been presented to the Queen as one of her bishops.

A cynical friend, who knew that I was dreading the possibility, told me that the thought just crossed his mind that I had criticised Charles so that such an appointment would be out of the question for me. In fact I had in any case told both the archbishops, as well as their appointments' secretary and the Prime Minister's, that at sixty-two I was too old, that I did not want it, and that I would only accept it if the Archbishop of York told me it was my duty to do so. Even so, I needed publicity like I needed a hole in the head.

Prince Charles's close friend and former equerry, Nicholas Soames, a junior Minister in the Major Government, was allowed (encouraged by Charles himself, so I was told) to break with tradition and attack me for what I had said, in the manner of a verbal horse-whipping inflicted upon an insolent peasant who had failed to doff his cap as the young master rode by on his sturdy mount.

Experience has taught me that one's fellow clergy are normally the most venomous in such circumstances, and revel in the opportunity to gain brownie-points by

attacking a colleague who has got himself on the wrong
side of episcopal authority.

On this occasion, it did not happen, with the exception
of a letter in *The Times* from the school chaplain at
Eton, the Revd. John Witheridge, who was once chaplain to the former Archbishop of Canterbury, Robert
Runcie. He doubtless pleased some readers by pointing
out my unsuitability to be Archdeacon of York. Whether
he would also have pleased his headmaster, Dr Eric
Anderson, is another matter. It was after all Dr Anderson
who urged recently that teachers should stand up for the
best and not pander to the lowest common denominator
in contemporary taste and manners:

> As guardians of civilised values, we must, like Old
> Testament prophets, tell people truths that they do
> not want to hear, that there are higher standards than
> those which most people find good enough, and that
> the effort to reach them is worthwhile.[1]

Clergy and bishops aside, letters from the general public
began to flow in, hundreds of them, with those in support
outnumbering those opposing by a ratio of four to one.
One theme occurred again and again: a despair at the
weakness of the bishops of the Church of England, at
the manner of their attacks on me, at their defence of
adultery ('a mere peccadillo' was one description). And
similar comments appeared in critical letters, with the
suggestion that the Church should put its own house in
order before attacking the royal family.

In defending the Prince, the bishops had been quick to
deny that private morality had anything to do with public
office. Unfortunately for men who like to run with the
tide, this time the tide was against them. Even more
unnerving for the bishops, a *Daily Mail* poll showed
an even greater distancing from the bishops' position
among young people and lower income groups, where

bishops do particularly like to believe they have their finger on the pulse of the nation. There was even worse to come as the government began to be beset by scandal, and bishops sought belatedly to acknowledge that maybe private morality was important.

Why should public reaction have been so strong at that moment in national life? I believe I did no more than set a spark to a fire which was about to burst into flame anyway. There had been a deepening of moral discontent at the explosion of petty crime, car theft, vandalism and the like, by apparently uncontrollable elements in some areas of our cities. Every day seemed to bring yet another horrific report of cruelty and random violence. The trial of two young boys for the murder of little James Bulger filled newspapers with a tale of such awful brutality that many could not bring themselves to read it. And perhaps it became too much.

Maybe it was the dawning of a realisation that the permissive Sixties, from which so much freedom was promised, had brought us as a nation to a bondage to sin from which we simply had to escape if society was to survive in any reasonable form. The alleged adultery of a prince of the realm or the admitted adultery of a minister of the Crown were merely symptoms of a deeper malaise. My comments on Prince Charles inadvertently became only one of a number of catalysts which started a debate which had become necessary in order to face the concerns which were in the minds of many people.

These anxieties were not primarily about the misbehaviour of the great and the not-so-good – though these were part of the wider picture – but about the quality of leadership we enjoy (or suffer) in Church and State, about the place of religious values and beliefs in our personal and public lives, and about the state of the nation in which we live and move and have our being.

This book will address some of those issues, and others which arise from them. The relationship between private morality and public office is clearly a major concern, and alongside that, the nature of Christian attitudes to ethical problems. The matter of leadership cannot be divorced from the place of the monarchy, and this must include the relationship between the Church of England and the Crown. Establishment must be considered alongside its alternative, disestablishment, and, with that, its effect on society. And if the private morality of public figures is relevant, is it relevant only for those in public life, or is it relevant for them because it is relevant for all of us?

There are no easy answers and this book will not offer them. But I hope it will open up questions which may help in the moral maze in which we presently find ourselves, in the light of the clear hope in the hearts of so many ordinary members of the public for a society better than the one we have inherited in 1995.

2

One Day's Problems – and Another's

So foul and fair a day I have not seen.
Macbeth, i.iii.38

Young men see visions but old men dream dreams. And it is the old man's privilege to complain that 'life isn't what it used to be in my young days'. Often it is no more than an ill-begotten nostalgia for a golden age which never really existed, a fantasy memory of long hot summer days, happy family outings with ne'er a cross word, ice cream, strawberry jelly, and egg sandwiches. 'We never had much money but we were satisfied with what we had.' The passage of time has expunged the pain of family quarrels, the hideously uncomfortable afternoons on rain-swept beaches, the greasy food in dirty cafés, a wintry discontent made glorious summer by kind forgetfulness.

But thirty, forty, fifty years ago, there *was* a stability and security which has since been lost. As one who came to teenage during the Second World War, the streets were surely safer than they are today, notwithstanding the possibility of air-raids. I could go to the cinema on a winter's evening and come home during the blackout without fear of molestation. My mother could collect the rents from my grandmother's nest-egg of back-to-back houses, with the danger of rape or mugging so unlikely as to be ignored. And if there were a robbery, it would be that and no more – not an occasion for an unprovoked and random knife attack bringing death or disfigurement.

One day's newspapers today tell a very different story. On 2 February 1994, I travelled from York to Dundee by rail to preach at a Candlemas service, with a longer-than-usual opportunity to read the papers in depth. There was the perennial story of car theft: a twelve-year-old boy on the run from a children's home who had then escaped from social workers at a court, stolen a car, crashed it after a police chase and been killed. At the time of his escape, he had been taking part in an activity programme on a narrow boat as 'punishment' for previous misbehaviour.

Then there was the incident where a motorist had stopped to help the victims of a fatal crash. As he tried to give aid to the casualties, one of the injured crawled away from the crash and stole the Good Samaritan's car. 'It really defies belief,' commented one of the police on the scene. But not nowadays, when anything goes.

Drugs have become a major cause of crime, and there was a report of the brutal murder of four innocent people on a holiday yacht in the Caribbean. But it was no ordinary murder, and a post mortem indicated that they had been tortured and beaten before being repeatedly stabbed in the face, head and neck. That was far away, yet only days later, paramedics on a drug-ridden estate in Manchester's Moss Side were issued with bullet-proof jackets as a safeguard from attack when they were performing their role of attending the injured.

In one paper on 2 February, a feature writer spoke of the 'flight from shame', citing evidence of the readiness of mistresses to profit from their affairs, of fathers unashamed at walking out on their families, girls unashamed at being single mothers, women unashamed at having babies by the husbands of other women. While the good side of such a change in values was more compassion and less judgmentalism, the bad side was that 'the failure to judge

and to condone certain ways of behaviour has led to . . .
a breakdown of individual responsibility'.[1]

Another story told of police who seized child pornography after thirty-one raids across the country, by which it was hoped a nationwide distribution network had been broken. The report added that in a twelve-month period, the Obscene Publications squad had confiscated 22,801 obscene videos, nearly 7,000 photographs and 43,452 obscene or indecent magazines. That this is probably merely the tip of the iceberg indicates the size of the problem. Maybe the much-ridiculed Mary Whitehouse had not been so wide of the mark after all in her long campaign against explicit sex and violence on television.

But as private morality had declined, it was no surprise that public ethical standards left much to be desired. MPs were reported to be asking why two former Foreign Office ministers, Lord Caithness and Mr Francis Maude, had 'blocked the release of key trial documents to a Malaysian banker detained in Britain who claimed he was being victimised by the Kuala Lumpur government'.[2] The two ministers had apparently issued immunity orders in 1990 and 1992 to prevent the use in court of documents which would have helped the banker in his trial. The report pointed out that similar immunity orders were used to suppress information in the Matrix-Churchill arms-to-Iraq trial, when innocent businessmen could have received long jail sentences as a result.

Only a week after the Public Accounts Committee had published a deeply disturbing report on standards in the civil service, the Comptroller and Auditor General complained that Whitehall reforms had led to corruption and waste on 'an unprecedented scale' being introduced into the civil service, as traditional public service values and rules were given little regard. Yet another report told of the trial of two health service officials and three businessmen who over four years had allegedly embezzled £400,000 from the NHS.[3]

Meanwhile, a father convicted of breaking the leg of a five-month-old baby and inflicting twenty-two other injuries during a six-week period was sentenced to eighteen months' probation by Judge Pryor, QC, and told to go on an 'anger-management' course. Sentencing the man at Bournemouth Crown Court, Judge Pryor told him: 'I am sure you lost your temper occasionally.'[4] Surely an understatement of gargantuan proportions even by today's standards on the judicial bench!

But the headlines were captured by President Clinton, who had ignored the advice of immigration officials and granted a visa to the Sinn Fein leader, Gerry Adams, allowing the IRA a propaganda coup against the British Government. The murderous and blood-soaked IRA campaign was carefully sanitised to gain the sympathy (and the dollars) of American audiences, with friendly television interviewers enrolled to give the best picture possible.

It is a characteristic of the weaker kind of liberal to be soft on terrorism, to be ready to be blind to the murder of the innocents which is the stock-in-trade of those who seek to gain their political ends by gun and bomb. Christians have no claim to clean hands: it was this same characteristic which led Christian churches and Church leaders in the 1970s and 1980s to embrace and give ready financial support to African liberation movements, and to ignore the brutality of the methods they employed to achieve their ends, however just those ends might have been.

And in the same way, we shall see later how Church leaders have all too easily espoused secular ideas and ideals at the cost of abandoning, or at least neglecting, the biblical principles which ought to have been the basis of any contribution to secular thought they might wish to make.

They are not the only cause of the declining standards of modern society. But they must bear a considerable burden of blame.

*   *   *

Four and a half months later, this book was nearing completion. On Saturday 18 June, the same exercise showed no change, no improvement, no indication that 2 February was a one-off day of depression.

The Glover family returned to their secluded house in West Yorkshire to find that the teenage girl who had been trusted with a house key (to feed the family cats) had, it was alleged, allowed friends to use the house for a wild four-day party, during which they had vandalised the house, stolen property, guzzled champagne, ruined carpets, and destroyed furniture.

Sgt Steve Powell who lives in Bromham, Bedfordshire, was recovering in a rehabilitation centre from an injury sustained at work. He returned home to find that a gang had torn up all his clothes, smashed his furniture, and poured oil over treasured family photographs, over his carpets and in his television set.

Little wonder that on the same day, Metropolitan Police Commissioner Sir Paul Condon attacked the public's 'Arthur Daley' attitude to crime, being unwilling to come forward as witnesses to crime, yet ready to buy goods with no questions asked. And the discredited Crown Prosecution Service was reported to have been instructed to get tougher with criminals. Instead of the criterion being that there would be a 'realistic prospect' of a conviction, the test should be 'when it is more likely than not' that a guilty verdict will be reached. In which case, a crime will be tested in the courts rather than decided by the criteria of the CPS.

A beggar – 'Homeless and Hungry' – was arrested and found to have a home provided and furnished by the taxpayer, together with a building society account into which he put his day's takings. Meanwhile, a beggar on the London Underground had been told by a passenger to 'get a job'. He was overheard by one Steven Burak, a man with a record of criminal damage and violence. He and the beggar followed the man on to a train, and assaulted him so severely that he needed four stitches in a head wound. Burak was arrested and eventually placed on probation. The magistrate, Quentin Campbell, told him:

> I am sure that you are normally a decent man. It was your concern for a person begging that brings you here. I agree that if a person is quietly begging and a passer-by makes remarks to him about getting a job, it can be very hurtful. You sympathised with that person, as I hope I would.[5]

Meanwhile, in Minehead a gang of fourteen-year-olds had been systematically tormenting an elderly couple. A long-serving police constable with an unblemished record caught one of them and cuffed him. In court, PC Guscott was fined for assault, and made to pay compensation to the boy by the magistrate, Lady Sarah Wright, sister of government minister William Waldegrave. Guscott was to face a disciplinary committee which could lead to his dismissal. A day later, it was reported that a gang of youths had taunted him while he was visiting a supermarket with his family.

But it was a traditionalist clergyman – who else? – who created a news story which promised to run and run. The Revd Peter Irwin-Clark, vicar of St James's Shirley in Southampton, has built up a large congregation, always holding firm to biblical doctrine and teaching scriptural moral standards. When two members of his flock left their respective partners and set up together as husband and wife, he encouraged them to repent and to return to their lawful husband and wife. When they did not do so, he invoked St Paul's injunction to the Christians in Corinth 'not to associate with any one who bears the name of brother if he is guilty of immorality or greed, or is an idolater, reviler, drunkard or robber – not even to eat with such a one'.[6]

In this he did little more than he is required to do by

the Book of Common Prayer if the congregation have been offended by a person's behaviour, where the person with the cure of souls must 'call him and advertise him, that in any wise he presume not to come to the Lord's Table, until he have openly declared himself to have truly repented and amended his former naughty life'.[7]

Such an excommunication might be condemned in today's Church as unchristian, but in St Paul's eyes it would be an act of charity preventing a sinner from eating and drinking God's judgment upon himself.[8]

But is the Revd Peter Irwin-Clark asking much more than the natural behaviour of most people? Few today have not had friends where husband and wife have separated because of the adultery of one of them. A husband who forsakes his partner and children for another woman may leave a family distraught and distressed, and needing all the help they can receive from friends. Almost always, old friends will rally behind one partner or the other and will tend not to continue a friendship with both separately as if nothing had happened. They may feel instinctively that to do so would be to condone the hurt imposed upon the deserted family.

For a church congregation to behave as if nothing had happened, welcoming the 'new' couple Sunday by Sunday alongside their two deserted families, would be as bizarre as it would be unchristian – unchristian because it would say in effect to the deserted husband and wife and respective children, 'Not only do we condone what has happened, but God supports them more than he supports you.'

It was interesting that many newspaper commentators saw it in this light, and rejoiced in the unexpected news of a Church of England clergyman demanding that moral standards be upheld. But not everyone was happy: the Revd J. H. Smith of St James's Breightmet in Lancashire wrote in a sneering letter to *The Times*:

If the Reverend Peter Irwin-Clark is going to get to Heaven, I will volunteer to go to Hell with Mr Goddard and Mrs Furby, his parishioners. It wasn't so much the sinners as the self-righteous who got up our Lord's nose.

So far as could be ascertained, the bishops were entirely silent on the issue. Of course, the exercise of leadership is not always or necessarily a public act; and sometimes when leadership is exercised publicly, it is less effective than the private action. Nevertheless there is a growing public feeling that society is rudderless, as violent crime appears to be on the increase and the values which make for a decent society are undermined or ignored.

3

Royal Affairs

> Yet such extenuation let me beg,
> As, in reproof of many tales devis'd,
> Which oft the ear of greatness needs must hear,
> By smiling pick-thanks and base newsmongers,
> I may, for some things true, wherein my youth
> Hath faulty wander'd and irregular,
> Find pardon on my true submission.
> Prince of Wales – *1 Henry IV, iii.ii.22*

Monarchs have not always been paragons of virtue, even though a few have been saints of God and so honoured in the Church's calendar. In pre-Conquest days, Edward became King of the West Saxons in AD 975 when he was about twelve years of age. Three years later he was murdered while visiting his half-brother, Æthelred, at Corfe Castle. It was a particularly brutal and teacherous murder by Æthelred's servants, who were doubtless intent on promoting their own young master to the throne. Æthelred, which meant 'noble counsel', was known by the nickname Unræd, which in contrast meant 'evil counsel'. He reigned from 978 to 1016.

Edward was notorious for his violent speech and behaviour, but in spite of this he was later canonised, probably more in penitence for the manner of his departure than for his own virtues. He is commemorated as St Edward, king and martyr, on 18 March.

Little is known of Edmund, probably a Saxon prince appointed by Offa to succeed him as King of the East Anglians. He was defeated in battle by the Danes, and is said to have refused to become a vassal prince unless the Danish prince became a Christian. For his obstinacy he was scourged and then fastened to a tree as a target for Danish archers. He was later canonised and his body transferred to the monastery at what is known today as Bury St Edmunds. His 'day' is 20 November.

Another Edward became king in 1042 and seems not to have been a particularly strong ruler at a time when one was desperately needed. He was keen only on hunting and religion, a tradition which more than a few country parsons have subsequently followed, and was responsible for the building of Westminster Abbey, which at that time was the most magnificent building in the land.

His claims to sainthood are unclear, but he was recognised for his devotion, gentleness and goodness in an age which was otherwise rough and cruel. He is celebrated as St Edward the Confessor on 13 October.

The only post-Conquest monarch to be given a date in the Church's calendar is Charles I. If Edward was a 'confessor' in the ecclesiastical sense – that is to say, he witnessed to, rather than died for, his faith – Charles was undoubtedly worthy of the title 'king and martyr'. Had he been willing to compromise with those who sought to destroy the ancient catholic roots of the Church of England, removing bishop and priest and adopting the presbyterianism of Cromwell and his cohorts, he would have saved his life.

But he was a godly man, whose faith was at the centre of his life, a faithful and loving husband, devout and careful in his religious duties. He met his death bravely, first spending hours in prayer and then receiving the Sacrament before stepping out from the Banqueting Hall in Whitehall on to the scaffold which had been prepared for him, and where he was beheaded.

After the Restoration, his name was included in the Calendar of Saints on 30 January, the day of his execution in 1649. It was removed without any authority by the printers of the Book of Common Prayer, when the service commemorating him was withdrawn by royal warrant in 1859. A number of churches are dedicated to him, and he is still commemorated on 30 January, mainly in places where there is a catholic rather than an evangelical tradition. Indeed one aspect of the crisis presently facing the Church of England is the desire of the powerful evangelical lobby to dispense altogether with the Book of Common Prayer of 1662, to allow lay presidency at the eucharist, and to remove the catholic understanding of a sacramental priesthood from Anglican theology. This would effectively reverse the ecclesiastical settlement agreed at the restoration of the monarchy (with Charles II) in 1660, and destroy the catholic roots of Anglicanism once and for all.

As well as those kings acknowledged as saints by the Church, other monarchs have been holy – sometimes more so than those canonised – and others good and honourable, qualities not always recognised in the holy.

Henry III succeeded his father, King John, in 1216, and his foreign politics were controlled by his commitment to the Crusades. It was a feature of the thirteenth-century ethos that the recovery of the Holy Land from the Saracen dominated men's thoughts and ideals, and was so much interwoven in everyday life that people and public events were inevitably affected by it. 'The call to the Crusade still sounded in the ears of men with remorseless iteration, to confuse or inspire the policies of princes. And . . . it confused no man more than Henry III, and inspired few men more than his son' (who was Edward I).[1]

But Henry was no weak king who neglected the affairs of state for the sake of the leadings of his faith, and the Treaty of Paris he concluded with his French adversaries ensured peace and friendship with France for thirty-five years, giving a breathing-space during which king and kingdom in England were united on a foundation of law and order which provided a much-needed stability in the troubled years to come. The commonly-expressed view that a morally and religiously good monarch is concomitant with being also a weak and ineffective ruler is certainly disproved in these two kings.

Nor is it the case that most monarchs have been immoral womanisers, at any rate in the case of those who reigned before the deplorable Henry VIII. Edward II's problem was certainly not with the opposite sex, and his infatuation with Piers Gaveston was a cause of much division within the state. Nevertheless he was married to the formidable Isabella of France, whose own lover, Mortimer, was eventually hanged, drawn and quartered. Edward himself was ultimately deposed and later murdered for incompetence, cruelty and wickedness, and a string of other charges.

His son, Edward III, succeeded, a vain and ostentatious man yet probably no more so than would have been expected of a monarch in those days. His wife, Philippa of Hainault, was later celebrated as a paragon among queens, 'a noble and good woman' who endeared herself to the people by her concern for the oppressed. Much is owed to her influence in the unity between royal family and State which she bequeathed to England. Her husband was no statesman: unscrupulous, untrustworthy, vain and dissolute, and before he was sixty he became senile, possibly affected by the dissipations of his earlier years.

But he did win and hold the affection of the common people, and his armies gained for themselves a great reputation by which Edward was perceived as the architect of England's fame and reputation after the degradations of his father's reign. His mistress, Alice Perrers, survived him, and her unpopularity, not least because of her influence during his declining years, led to her trial and the confiscation of her property.

If any king exemplifies the popular notion that immorality in personal behaviour is a prerequisite for one who is to be a strong leader, it is Henry VIII, and the manner of his leadership had one characteristic which populist leaders – monarchs, prime ministers, presidents, trade union leaders, bishops – will always emulate: he gave the people what they needed for confidence and self-respect. He was courageous, of a high intellect, with an instinct for rule which led his country through, and out of, difficulties which would have destroyed the kingdom of a lesser man. There might have been civil strife and if his cruelties served to prevent this, he was remembered as one who forestalled a return to the sufferings of the Wars of the Roses, held in the memory of the nation as surely as the brutal and senseless carnage of the First World War trenches is still a folk-memory after eighty years.

In his religion Henry VIII would always put himself before God, and his overriding principle was that of expediency. Throughout his reign he had never hesitated to remove any enemy whom he perceived as a threat to himself, and he did so in a manner which to us cannot but seem to be cruel, and as totally without humanity as any Nazi or Marxist ruler in this century. That it did not apparently seem so to the people of his day is a measure of the difference in their expectations.

Henry was an adulterer and a murderer, covetous and a thief, ready to bear false witness if this should be expedient, who behaved as if the King of England had God's exemption from the Ten Commandments. But he was a Tudor, and on the whole the Tudors were good monarchs for their own age.

After the restrictions of the Civil War and the imposition of Puritanism, it was perhaps inevitable that there would be a reaction of looser living. During the Cromwellian period, adultery had been punishable by death, swearing and drunkenness were attacked, fashions in clothes decried as mere vanity, Church festivals forbidden. It had all been too much to bear for the ordinary people, who were neither convinced royalists nor convinced parliamentarians. But a moral code imposed by a military dictatorship had within it the seeds of its own downfall. With the loss of the support of the ordinary people, the dictatorship fell, and in a bloodless revolution the monarchy was restored and the Church of England with it.

Moral standards at once relaxed, and relaxed all the more in reaction. Charles II and James II were firmly in that tradition. Charles's light-hearted infidelities were almost a relief to his subjects after the harsh morality of Puritanism, and even the more sombre irregularities of James II were accepted at first, before the question of his adherence to the religion of Rome became paramount.

It was with the accession of the House of Hanover (later of Windsor) to the British throne that there entered a different attitude to the moral life of the monarch. George I had had his wife, Sophie Dorothea, imprisoned for adultery with a man called Königsmarck, but comforted himself with no less than three mistresses. There was the Baroness Kielmansegge, eventually created Countess of Darlington, and the Baroness von Schulenberg (to whom he may have been married) who became Duchess of Kendal. In addition, there was also Madame von Platen, of the three the least unpleasing. Kielmansegge and Schulenberg became figures of fun to the general populace: the first for her height and scrawny figure nicknamed the Maypole, and the second, short and plump, was called the Elephant. Some say that it was these two ladies who were immortalised in the name of the South London public house, the Elephant and Castle.

George IV had been Prince Regent during the illness of his father, George III. Of some intelligence, he was interested in architecture and painting. His manner was pleasant or rude, as the mood took him. But he was a man much led astray into gambling and womanising by the politician Charles James Fox, so escaping into a world far away from the stultifying propriety of Windsor. In 1785 he had married, illegally, a Mrs Fitzherbert, but ten years later entered into a marriage (which Lord Malmesbury had negotiated) with Princess Caroline of Brunswick-Wolfenbüttel.

George disliked her intensely and wanted to be rid of her. In 1806 the government was forced to institute an enquiry into her conduct, and though charges against her were not proved, her reputation was gravely damaged. George III died in 1820 and when his son came to the throne he immediately began divorce proceedings against Caroline. The danger which the government perceived was that the Queen might bring counter-charges against the King, damaging his position from the start of his reign.

While Caroline made a triumphant entry into London – the people regarding her as a courageous and wronged woman – a bill was introduced into Parliament by which the royal marriage would be dissolved and the Queen deprived of her title, with a public enquiry into her conduct a necessary part of the procedure. It was thought likely that the bill would not pass the Commons, and so it was quietly dropped; and when Caroline accepted a pension of £50,000 a year and a house, she began to lose popular support.

However, the King was to be crowned in July and she claimed the right to be crowned with him as queen. As she was driven to Westminster Abbey with Lord Hood, she was cheered by the crowds lining the streets. But Lord Hood had only one entry ticket for the service and Caroline was refused admission. She died a month later.

William IV followed the Hanoverian tradition: he was married to Adelaide of Saxe-Coburg-Meiningen but faithful to Mrs Jordan, an actress. He had little constitutional power but his personal likes and dislikes caused him to interfere in politics, sometimes concerning the formation of ministries, and the source of much petty intrigue in government.

The House of Hanover has never been noted for intelligence or academic excellence, and constitutional monarchy is not capable of exercising the kind of influence on the affairs of state which the Tudors and Stuarts expected to enjoy. But careful study of official papers coupled with the experience gained during a long reign have enabled both Queen Victoria and our present Queen Elizabeth II to make significant if quiet contributions.

When Edward VII succeeded Victoria, it seemed like the dawn of a new age. His mother's self-imposed seclusion from public life was abandoned with Edward's conspicuous enjoyment of the pomp and pageantry of royalty. He was popular and this gave the impression of a new influence in the nation's affairs. It was not so in reality, for Edward lacked his mother's industrious determination to peruse all the official papers which came before her. He had champed at the bit as his mother's longevity kept him from the succession, and his many indiscretions made her reluctant to allow him access to confidential documents. Thus when he came to the throne, this necessary deprivation had left him without experience.

His marriage to the lovely but increasingly deaf Alexandra of Denmark was one of convenience, and he resorted to mistresses. It was said that royal blood now runs in the veins of not a few families in the Cambridge area as a result of fruitful liaisons made during the Prince's days at university, so having mistresses was nothing new in his life. But he was obviously devoted and perhaps faithful to at least one, Mrs Keppel, whom Queen Alexandra graciously allowed to be present at his death-bed. Mrs Keppel was the great-grandmother of Camilla Parker-Bowles.

It was his grandson, Edward VIII, who carried the Hanoverian instinct to its extreme. As Prince of Wales, he made popular excursions into areas of deprivation and sought a more adventurous royal involvement in national life. But he was feckless and like Edward VII would not prepare for his office by working at official papers. By the time of his accession in 1936 he had a consort, Mrs Wallis Simpson, whom he declared he would marry. Edward was forty-one years of age and still unmarried; Mrs Simpson was already married to Ernest Simpson, with another former husband still alive – and she was American and a commoner.

The King's personal friends were of a class totally out-of-touch with respectable opinion, and Mrs Simpson herself knew only the American code which took divorce more lightly than in Britain where it then carried a considerable social stigma. Moral standards had relaxed, but not so much as Edward seemed to imagine. Many public men may have had worse skeletons in their cupboards, but Edward would not be allowed to have his cake and eat it: he could not have the throne and Mrs Simpson. In the end he declared that he could not take the throne without the woman he loved beside him, and announced his abdication. His mother, Queen Mary, was horrified at what she saw as a dereliction of duty, even though she had once said that she hoped that nothing would in the end 'come between Bertie [George VI] and the throne'.

So Bertie did succeed in his brother's stead. George VI was a good and godly man, of whom it is said that on the eve of his coronation, crossed London alone from Buckingham Palace, wearing an old mackintosh and trilby hat. He knocked on the door of the Dean of Westminster and asked to be allowed into the Abbey to pray. When the Dean recognised who it was, he let in the King, who remained there alone for an hour, praying for strength and guidance in the task that lay ahead.

He could not then have guessed the magnitude of the task. Britain was on the verge of a world war against one of the most evil regimes of modern times, whose victory would have brought a new dark age of repression. His moral leadership at that time, with that of his queen, when it seemed at times that all was lost, was an inspiration and an example which ensured the royal family an unparalleled popularity in the nation. One can only speculate on what might have happened without the Abdication, with a King Edward VIII and Queen Wallis. It was certainly thought unwise to allow him to serve in the Army, and in 1940 and against his real wishes he became Governor of the Bahamas.

But Edward, whatever his past misdemeanours and whatever the marital state of his mistress, was himself unmarried at the time. His great-nephew, Charles, on the other hand is not only married, but married to a wife who is more popular by far than the Prince is himself. We cannot of course know the full truth of the alleged affair between Prince Charles and Camilla Parker-Bowles, nor can we know fully the causes which led to the breakdown of his marriage. His admission in the Jonathan Dimbleby television programme that he had been unfaithful to the Princess of Wales was qualified by the statement that this was only after the breakdown became irretrievable.

Any marriage goes through its difficult patches, and the difficulties are no justification for unfaithfulness, even though they may often be the cause. In any event, adultery is not the only expression of unfaithfulness in marriage. If the incidents recorded in Andrew Morton's book are true, then an intimate relationship continued between the Prince and his friend throughout the marriage, even if it was a relationship which for a period was not expressed in terms of physical sex. It could not but have contributed to the irretrievable breakdown of his marriage.

But constitutionally none of this can affect the succession. The moment the Queen dies, Charles will be king. 'The King is dead, long live the King' is a simple statement of fact. Prince Charles has many qualities which suggest that he would be an excellent King Charles III. He speaks out on issues which touch the public's own concerns – architecture and the environment, for example – and minority questions like organic farming and holistic medicine, which have a growing following.

Even so, the fact is that ten years ago, Prince Charles and Lady Diana Spencer exchanged solemn vows before God in St Paul's Cathedral in their fairy-tale wedding, promising lifelong faithfulness to each other. It was a fairy tale which, as we now know, quickly went sour. At his coronation, Charles would again be asked to make solemn vows to God to be faithful to his calling as a monarch, and to uphold the 'protestant reformed religion, established by law'. On 7 December 1993, I suggested in my comments on Radio 4 and in an article the next day in *The Times* that the question at least needed to be asked. If his attitude to his vows of matrimony, made in church and before God, was so cavalier, has he the right to expect to be trusted in this second solemnity?

The answer of course may be that the nation would trust him to do this, that attitudes to morality – and to matrimony – have so changed that faithfulness is an out-dated concept. If *The Times* leader were to be believed, that would have seemed to be the case: 'This so-called "moral argument",' it thundered, 'whatever the nature of the Prince's behaviour in marriage, is mischievous, fallacious, aggressive in language and wholly regrettable.'[2]

'Fallacious' was an unfortunate choice of adjective, since it is a technical term used in formal logic, the science of argument, which requires that my own assertions be subjected to a logical scrutiny. If the assertion is made into an 'all' proposition, it would read thus:

All vows made in church and before God by Charles will be honoured.
The coronation oath is such a vow.
Therefore it will be honoured.

His admission of unfaithfulness shows that we cannot

make such a proposition; but there is no evidence that we can use a 'no' proposition:

> No vows made in church before God by Charles will be honoured.
> The coronation oath is such a vow.
> Therefore it will not be honoured.

We are therefore left with a 'some are not' proposition:

> Some vows made in Church before God by Charles will not be honoured.
> The coronation oath is such a vow.

It would in terms of formal logic be 'fallacious' to move from the particular instance (in fact only one, the marriage vow) to a general statement:

> Therefore the coronation oath would be honoured.

But it would be equally fallacious to move from the particular instance to the other possible general statement:

> Therefore it would not be honoured.

The only logically valid statement which could be made which was not fallacious was in fact the one which I made:

> Therefore the coronation oath may or may not be honoured.

Or, as I put it, in the form of a question:

> If his attitude to his vows of matrimony, made in church and before God, was so cavalier, has he the right to expect to be trusted in this second solemnity?

The Times may be right to call this 'mischievous, aggressive in language, and wholly regrettable'. What it is not, and what it cannot be, is 'fallacious'.

The leading article went on to point out, correctly, that unlike a politician, a monarch is not elected or held accountable to a manifesto – but is 'a symbol of nationhood and history rather than the spokesman of a moral position' whose authority 'flows from proper allegiance to an institution rather than trust in an individual'. The presumption that a king should be 'a moral exemplar to the nation is a comparatively weak and recent one'.

That is certainly true and could hardly be otherwise, given the moral turpitude of not a few of Prince Charles's ancestors. Indeed, it is perhaps only since the Abdication of Edward VIII and the accession of the good and faithful George VI that this has become a characteristic and expectation of the monarchy, equally fulfilled in the present Queen.

The Times described what it called my 'equivalence of coronation and marriage vows' as crude, and suggested that 'a man whose marriage falters does not *ipso facto* become untrustworthy or incompetent'. Of course this is true – *ipso facto* – but there are varieties of marriage failure within that fact. A man whose wife walks out after twenty years of marriage because she can no longer bear the sight of him may indicate a long-faltering relationship, with blame on both sides. But neither partner can be deemed untrustworthy or incompetent. Or again, a couple who separate with no question of adultery with another on either side and who then remarry are in a different moral category from those involved, either or both, in adulterous relationships.

Love is a powerful emotion, and if, after years of a comparatively happy marital relationship, love dies in a marriage, it may be found elsewhere. But there is surely a qualitative difference between that and a marriage in which a relationship that had begun before the marriage

was continued in one way or another throughout the
marriage, in spite of promises of fidelity made to another
partner, in church and before God.

The Archbishop of York, in a *Times* article attacking
my own, supported the leader writer who disposed of
my 'fallacious argument that someone who broke their
marriage vows might treat lightly other vows, even those
affecting their primary vocation'.[3] Again there is the
careless use of the technical word, 'fallacious'. Yet in
a later article in *SeeN*, the York diocesan newspaper,
he admitted that the truest motive for refraining from
adultery is that it destroys fidelity and trust between two
people.[4]

If that fidelity and trust are broken systematically
throughout a marriage, without apparently any regard
for vows solemnly made – and received in honest and
loving trust by another – it would surely be a foolish
act on a future occasion to trust such a person's solemn
vow, executed before God. One broken trust may not
lead to another; but the question and the doubt must
be there, whether in buying a new car or in the taking
of solemn vows. The mischief and the fallacy is to suggest
otherwise.

However, in the latter part of his contribution,[5] the
Archbishop of York recognised that the public interest
in my comments came not so much from concern about
the royal family, as about the moral life of our nation –
that we are increasingly conscious of deep disorders in
our society, of a loss of moral direction. He ended by
expressing the hope that the debate might cause everyone
'to ask themselves how they measure up morally to their
roles', adding that if this happened it might – 'even at this
late stage' – do some good.

So far as the future of the monarchy and of the Prince of
Wales is concerned, it appears that the debate did indeed
do some good. Six weeks after the initial furore, it was
quietly leaked to a certain newspaper[6] that Prince Charles

had broken off his relationship with Camilla Parker-Bowles, for the sake of the monarchy and the succession. If it were true that Charles had realised through the public reaction that he could not abandon his wife for his mistress and still expect to retain the throne, such an announcement would not be made in a public statement, but through that all-embracing phrase: 'Sources close to the Prince of Wales have revealed . . . '

And that should be the end of the matter (as well as of the affair), especially for one who comments on the basis of Christian morality. The glory of the Christian gospel is that forgiveness and renewal follow repentance and amendment of life as surely as night follows day.

But ought there to be criticism by a Christian of another's behaviour?

4

Christians in Glass Houses

What was thy cause? Adultery?
Thou shalt not die: die for adultery! No:
The wren goes to't, and the small gilded fly
Does lecher in my sight.
Let copulation thrive.

King Lear, IV.vi.110

Some time after the Prince Charles episode, I was challenged over coffee after a church service by a woman deacon. How could I say such things? It transpired that she was not concerned with the accuracy of my comments about Charles, but at my lack of understanding of modern society. '*Everybody* commits adultery these days,' she declared. Well, I for one do not do so and never have done; nor I suspect have many of our friends. Nor for that matter do I believe for a moment that the woman deacon would have done so either. But it seemed to her sufficient justification for avoiding comment or censure of those who do.

The more frequent criticism came in letters I received reproving me for the remarks I had made. Many were from those who took the story of Jesus and the woman taken in adultery and applied it, literally but inaccurately, to what seemed to them to be the unedifying picture of a Christian minister attacking a member of the royal family for alleged adultery. At first sight their criticism appears entirely justified.

The story[1] tells how Jesus had been teaching in the Temple when a group of scribes and Pharisees brought a woman before him. She had committed adultery, 'caught in the very act'. What, they ask, does he say should be done to her since the law of Moses commands that she should be stoned? Of course it is a trick question since stoning to death was against the state law. This we know because when the Jewish religious leaders brought Jesus before Pilate for sentence, they told Pilate: 'It is not lawful for us to put any man to death.' But will Jesus insist that they hold to the law of Moses or the law of Rome? The conflict between the sacred and secular is part of the problem of religious leadership in today's secular society, but it is not the issue before us at present and must wait until later in this study.

The less intentional trick to the question is also at the heart of the Church's problem today in dealing with moral matters: to condemn or to condone? Jesus turns the challenge on the woman's accusers: 'Let him who is without sin among you be the first to cast a stone at her.' There is a pause as the men consider their own consciences and their own sinfulness, and then each of them, beginning with the eldest, goes away, leaving the woman alone with Jesus.

They have not condemned her, and, so the argument would go today, nor should Church leaders condemn sinners, but rather follow the example of the Jesus whom they are supposed to serve. Certainly an archdeacon ought not to condemn the Prince of Wales for alleged adultery. But nor did I: for condemnation in these terms is to be both jury and executioner.

In the story of the woman taken in adultery, God through Moses has set the law and is the judge of all things. And the law is clear: that a woman taken in adultery must be stoned, a punishment which the men are ready and willing to execute. As 'jury', they recognise her guilt, for she was 'caught in the very act', and this Jesus does not question – indeed, as a jury member, as it were co-opted by the scribes and Pharisees, he shares the recognition of her guilt, saying to her when all have left, 'Go, do not sin again.' The mistake of those who brought her before Jesus was that they wished to be her executioner as well as the jury which declared the law.

Elsewhere, Jesus gives a clear direction and warning against going a step further and taking the place of God as judge:

> Judge not, that you be not judged. For with the judgment you pronounce you will be judged, and the measure you give will be the measure you get.[2]

In other words, if we ourselves take on the role which only God can occupy, then we must expect, not the pure, absolute, perfect and utterly fair judgment which he would perform, but a defective judgment which would be inevitably be marred by our own imperfections.

We can parallel this in the dilemma which faced members of the General Synod of the Church of England when attempting to meet the problem of soaring divorce figures and the many requests which, as a direct result, parish clergy receive to conduct marriage services where one or both partners have been divorced.

Legally – that is, in the eyes of the State – such marriages may be solemnised. Indeed, one of the effects of there being an established church is that anyone who lives within the ecclesiastical boundaries of a parish has the right to be married in the parish church, regardless of church membership or even Christian affiliation. If the incumbent of the parish refuses, he is guilty of neglect of duty, and disciplinary proceedings may be taken against him in the ecclesiastical courts. But English law also gives Anglican clergy the dispensation to refuse, if they so wish, on conscientious grounds, to marry anyone within the lifetime of a former partner.

However, the Church's own rules are much more restrictive. In 1957, the Convocations of Canterbury and York laid down regulations on the axiom that remarriage after divorce, during the lifetime of a former partner, involves a departure from the principles of the Church. A clergyman should not therefore perform the Marriage Service in the case of a former partner still living. The fact that some do so means that they have made a choice between following the rule of the Church or exercising rights which exist under the secular law. The whole issue brings many problems of conscience for the clergy, and it would be wrong simply to dismiss their sincere attempts to grapple with a major moral and social problem of the day as no more than a choice between God and Mammon.

At the heart of their dilemma are the clear words of Jesus Christ: 'Whoever divorces his wife and marries another, commits adultery against her; and if she divorces her husband and marries another, she commits adultery.' This is the version in its earlier form in St Mark's gospel.[3] St Matthew softens it with the exception, 'except on the ground of unchastity',[4] and much ink has been spilled in arguing the validity, authenticity and implication of the so-called Matthean exception. Either way, the clear message of the one whom Christians are supposed to follow as the Word of God made flesh, is that to divorce and remarry, whether in all circumstances or in most, is to commit adultery.

Immediately preceding the statement recorded in St Mark, Jesus gives an even firmer injunction about the sanctity of marriage: 'What therefore God has joined together, let not man put asunder.' The Church has always a duty to act personally, with love and concern for those in its care; but it is not and has never been part of Western moral theology that to act pastorally, one must abandon clear principles and objective criteria.

It is these principles which the Convocation regulations of 1957 seek to acknowledge. But what of the marriage entered into without thought, or because a bride was pregnant, or where both parties soon realise they have made a dreadful mistake? Love can certainly die: but can the marriage itself die, so that the vows taken become in effect null and void? In an attempt to meet the pastoral needs of those who genuinely wish to make a fresh start, with a sincerity and determination which was not present in the first marriage, the Church of England's Synod has tried on more than one occasion to find a way through the maze which would meet the pastoral dilemma while at the same time affirming the lifelong commitment implied by the marriage vows.

This came to a head in debates in the early 1980s when seven possible options had been prepared, of which what came to be known as 'Option G' proved the least unacceptable. This involved judgments being made by bishops, or by advisory panels set up by them, on whether or not a particular couple seeking remarriage after divorce could or could not be allowed a marriage in church. Superficially it failed to gain the necessary support because the bishops were not trusted to act with uniform caution, as some might hold to the letter of the proposals and others allow all comers. Had Option G been adopted, it is highly probable that ten years later there would have been no restrictions whatsoever on remarriage after divorce.

But there was also an underlying unease which was probably even more important: that it became more judgmental to choose between couple A and couple B's situation than to have an overall policy which said that a clergyman should not perform the Marriage Service during the lifetime of a former partner – full stop. The bishop (in the terms by which we have considered the theological and moral implications of the story of the woman taken in adultery) would be required to act not only as jury and executioner but as judge also, with a wisdom and discernment which only God himself could possess.

In extreme examples, the case would not perhaps be too difficult to judge. A woman in her first marriage had suffered beatings and humiliation from her husband over many years until she eventually divorced him. Now she had met a fine man who would make a good and faithful husband and they were deeply in love. If some couples were allowed to remarry, it would not be difficult to see her as a proper candidate.

But suppose her former husband now sought to marry again, this time to a weak and submissive girl who already bore bruises on her face and arms, with the first wife (still living in a battered wives' refuge) having no plans to remarry? If a weak, over-liberal bishop in full possession of the facts had nonetheless given permission for a remarriage in church, the first wife might be forgiven for feeling that even God did not care that she had suffered so grievously.

Or suppose again that a man is allowed remarriage in church, having been unfaithful to his first wife almost from the honeymoon, while his former wife, who herself had remained faithful to her marriage vows, is refused by a stricter bishop? The wiser counsel would seem to be in both cases the opposite decision. Had the Synod accepted the proposals for Option G, a bishop would have needed the wisdom, not of Solomon but of God, to decide between one couple and another where the culpability within the first marriage was not so black or white, and the attitude to vows taken before God less cavalier. And the bishop and his advisers would have brought human imperfection to judgments which only God could safely make.

In the wider issues raised by the story of the woman taken in adultery, part, but only a part, of that imperfection may be our hypocrisy, the blindness to our own sin which not only impairs our ability to judge others but brings a greater condemnation upon us:

Why do you see the speck that is in your brother's eye, but do not notice the log that is in your own eye? Or how can you say to your brother, 'Let me take the speck out of your eye', when there is a log in your own eye? You hypocrite, first take the log out of your own eye, and then you will see clearly to take the speck out of your brother's eye.'[5]

It was to the 'log in the eye' that Jesus drew attention when he told the scribes and Pharisees, 'Let him who is without sin be the first to cast a stone at her.' Far from abrogating the demands of the Law of Moses, Jesus in fact sharpens them:

You have heard that it was said, 'You shall not commit adultery.' But I say to you that every one who looks at a woman lustfully has already committed adultery with her in his heart.[6]

It may well have been an owning of this common instinct in the heterosexual male that caused the woman's accusers to go away, 'beginning with the eldest', when challenged by Jesus about their own sin. But the challenge in fact was not 'Let him who has not even committed adultery in his heart cast the first stone', but 'Let him who is without sin . . . ' The men's acknowledgment of their own sinfulness was, importantly, not confined to any sins of the flesh they might have committed or contemplated, but rather of the reality that all had fallen short of the standards set by the One who is the only Judge.

In the moral field, the mistake which is so damagingly made by many Church leaders and spokesmen today, on the basis of a false interpretation of the story of Jesus and the woman taken in adultery, is a two-fold one. On the one hand, there is the failure to make the distinction between judge, jury and executioner. Only God can judge us for the culpability we must bear for the sins we commit, but if we are not prepared to 'name' the sins we see around us (recognising at all times the sins which so easily beset each one of us), then we must bear the blame if society ceases to care for God's law.

On the other hand, there is the implication of the words by which Jesus sends the woman away: 'Go, do not sin again.' It is a small step from the failure to 'name' sin to condoning it, and it is this exclusion which has caused so much damage in recent years to the Church's witness to society. If we are free from blame for that which we do wrong, then moral behaviour quickly ceases to be a desirable goal.

Perhaps not surprisingly, I was much involved in the media debate which developed at the time of the Dimbleby programme on the Prince of Wales. It was a good opportunity to put forward to a very wide audience the simple but glorious truth that is the heart of the gospel: that after repentance and amendment of life, God washes the slate clean and we have a fresh start. But I felt that I was appearing too often, either in print or on television and radio, and I frequently suggested they should try to get someone else.

But none of the bishops would speak out, and as we shall see later, this was probably on instructions from on high.

As a result of this frequent and common hesitation, it sometimes seems that the flaccid moral leadership given by the Church in recent years, in its desperation to appear relevant and credible to a society overtaken by the *mores* of the 1960s has passed beyond the point of renewal and restoration. Even government ministers sometimes bewail that lack of leadership by the Church.

But woe betide a Church leader who does make a moral statement, be it against political behaviour or royal misdemeanours. And the greater denunciation of the spokesman who steps out of the line will come not from the State but from the Church itself.

5

Faith, Grace and Truth

My bounty is as boundless as the sea,
My love as deep; the more I give to thee,
The more I have, for both are infinite
                    Romeo and Juliet, ii.ii.133

The avoidance of the temptation to act as judge, jury and executioner is only part of the challenge which the Christian gospel lays upon its adherents in facing up to the actions of others that fall short of the ideal set by God, what in other words the Bible calls sin.

A few weeks after the Prince of Wales episode, a journalist from one of the Sundays – I think the *Mail* or the *Express* – telephoned me to say that friends of Charles had 'let it be known' that the Prince had given up Camilla Parker-Bowles for the sake of the monarchy. Would I comment?

'If he's done that, then that's all that is necessary,' was my reply. He seemed puzzled, as if it were to be expected that an apparently hard-line, moralistic clergyman would demand that the future king should don sackcloth and ashes, and crawl on hands and bare knees from Buckingham Palace to Westminster Abbey. But after all, when Jesus saw that none of the leaders of the Temple had acted as executioner by casting the first stone against the woman, he simply said to her, 'Go, do not sin again.'

Of course in human terms, it is all quite unfair, as a modern rendering of Jesus's story of the Prodigal Son[1] illustrates:

A certain man had two sons, Shimon and Yakob. The younger, Shimon, was resentful of the way his father treated him, ever critical, apparently ungenerous, and one day he asked to be given his share of the family fortune.

His father tried to argue: 'You'll waste it all if I do.' 'No, I won't,' the son replied. 'But what I will do is to show you that I am just as capable as my brother, that in a few years I'm a good enough businessman to make it into another fortune.' So his father tried another route: 'What about your mother? It will kill her if you leave. Why can't you find a nice Jewish girl to marry? Settle down, raise sons of your own. Be like Yakob.'

But the boy was adamant: he had had enough and he was determined to leave. So his father gave him a large sum of money and he went to a far country. At first he genuinely planned to set up a business, even thought out what it would be. But first, just a bit of excitement – a nice flat, get some expensive transport, join an exclusive club, something to attract friends in a strange country. And the friends came, and the women, and Shimon developed expensive tastes in entertainment, in heavy gambling, excessive in every way that his new friends encouraged him.

He soon realised the money was now much less than his father had given him. But there was still enough, even if the business would not be quite so big and the fortune would take longer to make. Just another six months' pleasure, then another three, then another one, then the money was gone. With it went the woman, the friends, the lifestyle. He was penniless, jobless, friendless and a long way from home in a strange country.

Hungry, Shimon tried for this job and that, but he was homeless, scruffy and a bad risk all round. In the end, in despair, he took work with a pig farmer, ill-paid and only able to afford to eat what the pigs had left of their own meal. Pigs, the unclean animal, untouchable and uneatable for a good Jew.

Then he had an inspiration. 'What a fool I am!' he said to himself. 'My father's servants are better off than I am. He's a good man – and a soft touch. I know what I'll do – I'll go home and say to him, "Father, I've sinned against heaven (must put that in – he's always at the synagogue) and against you. I'm no longer worthy to be your son, I know, but please give me a job and I'll work as one of your servants."' So he began the long hard journey home, practising all the time his set speech of half-apology.

So far so good: he has turned his back on the good-for-nothing life which he had been leading and he is returning home to the better values of his family. That is not to say he is sorry for the way he has behaved, and that given another slice of the family fortune he would not return at once to the far country to begin again where he had left off. He is sorry for the mess he is in, and little more than that. And human justice and human compassion seem to demand that the story should continue something like this:

When Shimon was still a great way from home, his father's manager saw him and told his employer, 'It looks as if that son of yours is on his way back. I expect he's broke. What do you want me to do? Shall I send him on his way?' Shimon's father was angry and a little sad at his manager's harshness.

'Whatever he's done, Shimon is still my son. Let him in the house and show him to my office. But keep him guessing – don't make him too welcome,' ordered the

father. The manager did just that and eventually, after
an anxious time outside the door, Shimon was invited
into the office.

For a moment the father kept his head down, writing.
Finally he put down his pen, looked his son firmly in the
eyes. 'So what have you to say for yourself?'

'Father,' said Shimon, 'I know I have been a fool. I
have sinned against heaven and before you and I'm no
longer worthy to be called your son. But please give me
a job and I'll work very hard as one of your servants.'
By now he had practised the little speech so many times
that even to Shimon it sounded weak and inadequate.

His father smiled. 'Of course I'll give you a job.
You're my son and I love you. What sort of a father
would turn his son away? And I'll tell you this, that if
you work hard, you could reach the highest position in
the firm if you're the best at the job – but no favouritism,
mind! What you've done, the money you've wasted,
the sins you've committed, I won't hold any of it
against you.'

Shimon wept at his father's kindness, and even his
brother Yakob was pleased: 'Shimon, Shimon,' he said,
'are we not fortunate to have so good a father, who
forgives us for whatever we do?'

But in fact that is not how the story of the Prodigal
Son ends; and St Paul does not speak of faith, hope and
niceness ('and the greatest of these is niceness') but of
love, which is a much harder taskmaster. For what really
happens is this:

While Shimon is still a great way from home, his father
sees him in the far distance and rushes to meet him
where he is. Shimon manages only to get out the first
part of his half-hearted excuse, and the father brushes
it aside as he organises the welcome, for his son was
lost and is found, dead and is alive.

'You go quickly and get a coat for him, clean clothes, shoes for his feet – anything he needs. And you, go and get food – yes, kill the fatted calf, we'll give him a meal to remember.'

Yakob, his elder brother, is not pleased – in fact he is very angry. 'Why are you doing this for your good-for-nothing son? I've served you faithfully all these years, never putting a foot wrong, never wasting your money, never chasing other women. When did you show me this kind of love?'

'When did I show you my love, Yakob? Why, all the time. But you were always trying so hard to make me love you that you could never see it.'

And that is the point: we simply do not need to try to earn the love of God. The danger is that we almost imagine a ladder set between us and the Father. We clamber up a few rungs and because, by reason of the failings in our humanity, we quickly fall to the bottom again, we say, 'Sorry, God. Please forgive me and I'll try harder next time.' And the more we try, the harder we fall.

The difficult lesson to learn is that it is only when we acknowledge not only our sin but our weakness too, when we say, 'Sorry, Lord, I can't do it on my own but only with your help,' that he is able to lift us to himself, restored, redeemed, sanctified. We are then, as St Paul says, 'accepted in the beloved'.[2] For the fact is that God accepts us as we are and where we are, not because this good act is balanced against that bad one, not because by our good works we have wormed our way into his favour.

The younger son, Shimon, practised his little speech to please his father but it was brushed aside as the father met him half-way – even though the young man was more sorry for himself than for the sins he had committed, ready if given half a chance to do it all again, and perhaps not even aware of the hurt that some of his actions had given his father.

St Paul's great phrase, 'by grace you have been saved through faith . . . it is the gift of God',[3] is the heart of the Christian message – that God restores us to a right relationship with himself, a relationship broken by sin; that he will maintain that relationship, if only we ask, by the grace he offers to us, and that this is not for any good works on our part but simply because we have the faith to seek it and the trust that it will be given. It is God's free gift. It can be rejected; but it cannot be bought.

It means that Jesus could declare to the thief dying next to him on another cross, 'Today you will be with me in Paradise.' Here was a robber who had admitted that he was receiving no less than his crimes deserved, yet who in the excruciating pain of his execution showed a little act of kindness to the innocent Jesus dying next to him, by saying: 'Here, mate, you remember me when you come into that kingdom you've been going on about!' The answer was more than he could have bargained for: 'Truly, I say to you, today you will be with me in Paradise.'[4] Paradise? After all his evil deeds? For no more than a kind word? Well, that was what the man said.

The light of love which Jesus detects in the penitent thief on the cross is faint and dim, hardly able to overcome the darkness surrounding it. But it is enough, as it was for the woman taken in adultery in the abject terror of what she thought was to come, as it was for the paralysed man brought to Jesus on a stretcher whom he ordered to show that his sins were forgiven, 'Rise, take up your bed and go home,'[5] as it was for the young man whose father met him in love while he was 'still a great way from home'.

That the love of the father comes while the sinner is 'still a great way off' is a recognition not only that everyone falls far short of the perfection demanded by God, but also that part of the imperfection is that we are unable often to recognise the reality of where we have fallen short. The gift of God is not merely that we are accepted at the point at which we acknowledge we can only succeed in his strength rather than our own: it is also that we are accepted for the sins and failures of which we are not even aware.

Moreover, the sins are not just forgiven but remitted, and one of the weaknesses of the eucharistic prayers in the Alternative Service Book is that, unlike the Book of Common Prayer which uses the phrase 'remission of our sins', they speak of the blood of Jesus 'shed for you and for many for the forgiveness of sins'. Forgiveness is a human act which says in effect: 'You have hurt me by your unkind words or wicked action, and neither of us can undo what has been done. But I will put it out of my mind and behave as if it has never happened.'

Remission, on the other hand, is a divine accomplishment by which the sin is removed as if it had never been. Forgiveness writes the word 'SIN' and crosses it out; remission wipes the slate clean.

This is so clearly the message of the gospel of Jesus Christ, the good news which offers hope to all, that it is difficult to comprehend the blindness of those modern liberal theologians and Church leaders who seek always to minimise or even remove the reality of sin. The Revd Hugh Dawes, vicar of St James's Cambridge, wrote recently of the 'orgy of monstrously masochistic self-denigration' with which Christian worship is riddled, constantly demanding the confessions of sins rather than rejoicing at human good. Dawes sneers at the 'celestial rescue operation performed through Jesus which is proclaimed as having put things right'.[6]

There was once a phrase, which I understand is now unfortunately omitted, in the Bidding Prayer which opens the Festival of Nine Lessons and Carols broadcast each Christmas from King's College Chapel, Cambridge, inviting us to remember 'all those who know not the lord Jesus, or who love him not, *or who by sin have grieved his heart of love*' (emphasis added).

When by sin we fall short of God's ideal, we 'grieve

his heart of love' and there is the need to put that right. The fundamental point which Dawes and his supporters altogether overlook is that in admitting our failures before God in worship, we simply do not have to indulge in 'an orgy of monstrously masochistic self-denigration' or anything which approaches it. To confess one's sins is for the Christian not to grovel before an unforgiving, demanding deity requiring his pound of flesh, but the most joyful recognition of an acceptance offered by a God who is Love itself.

Few of his fellow-believers would go so far as Dawes in removing the promises and effects of God's love for his children which is the Christian gospel. But the diminution of a sense of sin does seem to be an important item on the agenda of liberal Christians – save of course for the politically correct condemnation of such corporate sins as racism, classism and sexism. The damaging effect of all this is to transfer the responsibility for wrongdoing from the individual to society or 'the government' or 'the system'.

This is precisely the sin of Adam and Eve in the Genesis story.[7] God tells them they may eat of the fruit of all the trees in the Garden, save that of the tree in the midst of the Garden. The serpent tempts Eve by suggesting God has lied: 'Has God told you that you will die? You will not die. What will happen is that you will be like gods knowing the difference between good and evil.' So the woman eats the fruit and gives her husband the fruit to eat as well.

When they hide from the Lord God, he realises what they have done: 'Have you eaten of the fruit of the tree which I forbade you to eat?' 'Actually, it was my wife's fault,' Adam replies lamely, the first husband to blame his wife. And, more aggressively, he turns on God: 'In fact, it was the woman you gave me, so it's your fault too. Don't try to blame me.' Eve simply pins the fault on the serpent who tempted her.

It is the human characteristic of refusing to accept

responsibility for one's own actions that marks the modern attitude to sin within liberal Christianity, overturning scriptural teaching from the very first pages of the Bible. It is the root of a deep malaise within our society, and a failure of leadership with consequences which, since we do not have the benefit of hindsight, are perhaps more far-reaching than we can now see.

Certainly there is much pressure to see biblical moral teaching as something which was culturally conditioned by the age in which Old and New Testament leaders – Jesus included – lived, and to suggest that with the benefit of twentieth-century understanding, we can discard that which is contrary to the accepted moral understanding of our age. It is a new morality which is only a little removed from the old immorality.

6

A New Morality and a New God?

Commit the oldest sins in the newest kind of ways.
2 Henry IV, iv.v.124

It was in 1963 that John Robinson's book, *Honest to God*, burst on an unsuspecting world, initially serialised in a Sunday newspaper. It was an instant success in a decade which prided itself on its iconoclastic propensities and it rapidly became an unlikely best-seller. Its author, Dr J. A. T. Robinson, had formerly been a Cambridge don, but at the time of the book's publication had been suffragan Bishop of Woolwich in the diocese of Southwark for some four years.

Of his book, Robinson commented at the time that 'it will seem to be radical, and doubtless to many heretical. The one thing of which I am fairly sure is that, in retrospect, it will be seen to have erred in not being radical enough.' Thirty years later, it can be said that for some the latter assessment is certainly true, and within the Church of England it is fair to say that not a few of our theological schools are dominated by teaching which is far more radical than the hesitant heresies chronicled by Robinson in *Honest to God*.

Robinson himself was a scholar of great integrity and honesty. He was not one of those, polemicist rather than scholar, who would come to a radical conclusion and then search for such evidence as might support it, while carefully excluding any invalidating testimony. Later in his career, when he had returned to the academic life to which he was more suited, he published in 1976 one of his finest studies, *Redating the New Testament*, in which he came to the conclusion that the whole of the New Testament was written before AD 70.

One reviewer noted that this overturned the judgments of most New Testaments scholars throughout the world, raising 'serious if unfashionable questions'. But Robinson was never concerned to be fashionable, and in *The Priority of John*, published posthumously in 1985, he argued persuasively and controversially that the gospel of John was the first to be written, pointing to a direct authorship by John himself. It did not endear him to his fellow New Testament scholars, but Robinson would never postulate a 'popular' solution if his scholarship led him to a different conclusion. He was a pure and incorruptible radical and a liberal in the true sense of that much misused word. He was a rare bird in the academic world of his day, of a *genus* which today seems almost extinct.

Robinson did not create the concept of a 'new morality' but rather he examined and distilled thoughts and ideas set out by scholars such as Emil Brunner and Paul Tillich. But he did give it a popular form, and if any one person can lay claim to introducing the new morality to a wider public, it has to be John Robinson.

It is an ethic centred – attractively – on love.

> Love alone, because, as it were, it has a built-in moral compass, enabling it to 'home' intuitively upon the deepest need of the other, can allow itself to be directed completely by the situation.[1]

Situation ethics is an ethic of 'radical responsiveness' which meets every situation openly and only on its own merits, without any prescriptive laws, without any religious moral code, free for ever to respond to the immediate situation:

> It is prepared to see every moment as a fresh creation from God's hand demanding its own and perhaps wholly unprecedented response.[2]
>
> It is a radical 'ethic of the situation', with nothing prescribed – except love.[3]

Robinson regards it not as a new morality, but simply as none other than the old, with an emphasis on the commandment to love one another. He compares it to St Augustine's famous dictum, '*Dilige et quod vis fac*': 'Love and do what you please',[4] which he suggests correctly translated should read, 'Love and then what you will, do.'

In situation ethics, that we care enough for another is the basis of ethical behaviour rather than the setting of rules and prohibitions. Love, caring, is the criterion for every form of behaviour: 'for *nothing else* makes a thing right or wrong'.[5] Unfortunately for the Christian, this ignores the need to see the place which law had in the mission and teaching of Jesus, who came not to abolish the law but to fulfil it: 'For truly, I say to you, till heaven and earth pass away, not an iota, not a dot, will pass from the law until all is accomplished.'[6]

Moreover, in practical terms, to claim that how we love someone is all that matters, that 'nothing else makes a thing right or wrong', is to disregard the reality of the human condition. St Paul, who understood human nature better than we would often give him credit for, expressed it well when he said of himself: 'I can will what is right, but I cannot do it. For I do not do the good I want, but the evil I do not want is what I do.'[7]

The ideal which Robinson describes is persuasive and laudable; but it is an ideal which founders on the rock of human nature. If we could truly say, 'I behave like this towards you because I love you,' and say it in full awareness of any hidden motives or desires – that is, if we could see ourselves as only God can see us – then a situation ethic based only on love might work. It might produce a society where each cared for the other, utterly, totally and dispassionately, a society where there was no violence, no exploitation, no abuse.

But life is not like that and we are not like that. If we were, there would have been no need for the Cross, no place for redemption, no understanding that God can bring us to himself and make us what he intends us to be only when we commit ourselves totally to him. It was a concept which was intended to be a force for good and instead became one of the factors in the terrible decline of values which has so damaged the quality and decency of human existence in our Western society.

Robinson's situation ethic came at precisely the wrong time. Love was the byword of the Sixties generation, yet that was a decade which proved almost totally destructive of common values, from bad architecture constructed from the shoddiest of materials to the abandonment of moral standards, all in the name of a spurious freedom and in favour of a shoddiness of life from which we still seek to recover.

In a booklet produced to introduce the Church in Canada to delegates at the 1983 Vancouver Assembly of the World Council of Churches, Rodney Booth inadvertently hit the nail on the head when he wrote:

I loved the 1960s! The nation's campuses were alive with student unrest. Even our music promised a brave new world ('We shall overcome,' 'If I had a hammer,' etc). Nowadays the only way to provoke a student revolt would be to increase the price of hamburgers in the college cafeteria. And it's hard to rally the troops around some contemporary country music epic like 'Drop-kick me, Jesus, through the goalposts of life'.[8]

Humanity does need a freedom to be itself, and the God-given gift of free will is an acknowledgment of this. When we were made in the image of God, we received two gifts unique in creation: the power to love and the power to choose between doing good or doing evil. That is a freedom which we constantly misuse, and it seemed in the Sixties that this very freedom, the freedom to sin, was offered as the liberation needed for humanity to reach its full potential. It was a modern version of serpent's temptation in the Garden of Eden:

'Did God tell you that you were not to do anything which you might find enjoyable?'

'No, not so. We may do many things which are enjoyable, but we may not break the commandments of God lest we displease him.'

'You will not displease him. He wants you to find your full potential as human beings, and you can only do this by experiencing all aspects of life, by enjoying every possibility which comes your way.'

But the reality is that God's commandments are not arbitrary whims of a rather unpleasant divinity, bent on spoiling life's little pleasures. They are the means of achieving a good society. We need a spiritual basis to life, with an awesome wonder at the fact of creation which points us to a loving, caring Creator outside ourselves, to whom we know we must turn for strength, a God whom no other gods must replace. If we dishonour parents, if we murder, if we commit adultery, if we steal, lie or covet, we help to create a society where life is not worth living, where human potential is debased and degraded from what it might have been.

The moral understanding together with the demand for a false freedom which has developed in the past three decades, far from increasing love and the quality of society, has done immeasurable damage. But there is a third factor which again began from a justifiable aspiration: the emphasis on human rights. It is right to call it a 'justifiable' aspiration, and it has been entirely proper for those concerned with the ethics of a good society, inside the churches as well as outside them, to seek to promote human rights, especially in a world where they are so often denied.

Brave men and women have given life and liberty in Soviet Russia, Communist China, in South Africa, in South American dictatorships, in their fight for basic human rights in those countries, and the churches have often shared in their struggle. There have been notable successes, and it would have been deemed an absurd prediction only a few years ago to have suggested that the communist empire would by now have collapsed or that Nelson Mandela would be president of a multi-racial South Africa. So other history hints that one day the tyranny in China will also end.

Unfortunately the concept of human rights has been adopted as a much wider slogan, and with it a diminution of its necessary corollary, responsibility. The demand for rights at the expense of responsibilities has been the root of much misery.

One of the most serious in its effects has been the emphasis in the abortion debate on the woman's human right to choose what happens to 'her own body', without regard for the rights of the human life developing in her womb. The killing of an unborn child has been sanitised by its depersonalisation, described as 'merely' a foetus rather than as a human child with the full potentiality to develop into nothing other than a mature human being. The woman's right to choose has been used to deny the baby's right to live.

The desire to give the mentally disabled and education-ally sub-normal a right to live in the wider community, to be taught in 'normal' schools, to look after themselves in their own homes – at first sight comprehensible and praiseworthy – in reality often denied them the care which was also their right and which it was the responsibility of the more able to provide for them. In the process, the security of the 'faceless institution' – the home they knew and could cope with – was taken from them, and they were thrown into a community where they found they were often unable to cope. In providing a human right which most share, their right to be given the appropriate kind of care for their particular needs was denied, and an avoidable social deprivation was the result.

Those who commit crimes possess human rights – to be fairly tried whatever their means, to be humanely treated if imprisoned, to be sentenced with leniency or severity according to circumstance. But society also has the right to expect to be protected from those who, by their actions, or crimes, would take away the wider human right to live in a safe and peaceful community. It is a proper cause of concern today that the rights of the victim have been undermined in the face of pressure to protect the rights of the criminal.

Society should expect the police to be beyond reproach in their methods as well as in their treatment of the criminals whom they bring to justice. Evidence should not be planted or manufactured, and prisoners must not be beaten or threatened to persuade them to confess or give evidence against another. Justice must be seen to be done and police who break the rules must be severely punished. But the protection of the human rights of criminals appears sometimes to take precedence over the responsibility of society to give the police force, which acts only on its behalf, all the support it requires in fulfilling its task. Instead, the police often seem hamstrung by the restrictions placed upon them, and the criminal's victim becomes a casualty for a second time.

The judiciary appears to be afflicted with the same disease, and it seems that almost weekly a horror story is told of a criminal laughing at the absurdity of the sentence imposed upon him. In such a society, where we no longer have faith in the wisdom of either judge or jury, it is only a small step to instant judgment and the lynch mob.

Church leaders are remarkably and strangely silent in the face of clear evidence of serious moral decline. As we shall see in the next chapter, they do often give a lead on social issues with a moral content, but their contribution is often tempered by political considerations which cripple the Christian content. But to deny the absolute in moral issues, as they sometimes seem to do, is to encourage a moral relativism which serves only to encourage those who would wish to set aside the concept of sin, and at the same time fall into the fundamental error of supporting individual rights so exclusively as to lead to the abandonment of personal responsibility. The result can only be a greater dis-ease in our society.

The easy solution would be simply to suggest that we return to a biblical morality and a firm discipline to enforce it. Certainly the achievement of a proper alliance between human rights and human responsibility is a necessary step along the way; and if society could learn that the precepts which Jesus taught, together with a commitment to the rules embodied in the Ten Commandments, are the good foundation for a just society, the balance so disastrously lost in the past thirty years might begin to be redressed.

Unfortunately we are also a society which has lost a sense of the divine, an awareness that there is a spiritual realm which points us to what we might become. The statement which St Paul makes in his letter to the Ephesians, 'By grace you have been saved through faith . . . it is the gift of God,'9 is at the heart of our need, for it embodies the four essentials: faith, grace, salvation, and the recognition that this comes only from God, and comes as a free gift. It is a gift offered out of love, without conditions and without the requirement on us to work our way into his favour.

This is so far from the teaching offered by some modern liberal theologians as to be deeply disturbing. The most extreme view is set out in a book already quoted (p.44), *Freeing the Faith*, by the Revd Hugh Dawes, a priest in Cambridge. The case he sets out deserves to be treated with the utmost seriousness, although not because it is remotely compatible with orthodox Christianity. It is important because the new theology which is presented is, I am convinced, widely held and taught – held by many clergy if not publicly taught by them, and disseminated assiduously in some of our theological colleges and on many of our non-residential ministerial training courses.

I was invited by the publishers of *Freeing the Faith* to engage in public debate with Hugh Dawes on the contents of his book, and I said this:

But first listen to the respect in which Hugh Dawes holds his opponents. 'The claims the orthodox make for themselves and their ideas are nonsense,' he says. 'The traditionalist view is unlovely and repellent', the gospel we proclaim a 'tragic irrelevance', and prayer 'the mumbo-jumbo of superstition', all of which would, he suggests, be 'laughable, were it not so tragic'. We are 'blinkered and sectarian', and dredge up 'the detritus from the Christian rubbish heap'. Christian ministers are 'like the witch-doctors of other cultures': we are 'traders in heavenly promises' who call upon our 'followers to deny their experience in an orgy of monstrously masochistic self-denigration', and require them to 'swallow six impossible things before breakfast'.

He sneers at conservative Christianity for 'treating the Bible as the ultimate User's Book of Life', and evangelism as 'religious recruiting'. He has utter contempt for the 'pathetic gaggles of Christians gathered at shopping centres at Christmas or on Good Friday, apparently in order to make people feel guilty', mocking their attempt at witness and distorting their motivation.

Fortunately, those of us who are accustomed to challenging the liberal establishment know that this kind of abuse is their stock-in-trade, acceptable only to their supporters and quite properly off-putting to everyone else. So too is the distortion with which he presents, and then dismisses, the orthodox position.

For example, he suggests that we 'claim faith is above reason and inaccessible to reason'. Not true: we value the Anglican triumvirate of scripture, reason and tradition, though certainly within that we give primacy to scripture. Indeed, one of the fundamental differences between orthodox and – to use Hugh Dawes's own description – open believers is that the latter appear to give primacy not to scripture or tradition but to reason.

He quotes critically a writer who claims that 'if Jesus was not more than a man, then the whole Christian faith and all the generations of Christian worship have been one monstrous, deluded idolatry'. Dawes comments: 'Outside the camp of biblical fundamentalists . . . I doubt whether such arguments truly count for much.' So the orthodox are lumped together as fundamentalists for their faith in the incarnation.

Speaking of the Church, he says that 'the idea today that there is merit in the church being a wholly isolated community, guarding and enclosing truth that owes nothing whatsoever to that world is something very recent'. I am bound to say that it is so recent that I have yet to encounter it.

Nor do I recognise his description of Christianity itself:

Christianity is taken to be at heart about the promise of life *beyond* the material mode of our present existence; salvation is from the world rather than in it. In the short term, and just for the time being, the role of the church is to keep people safe and unharmed, cocooned against the forces said to be lurking outside, until death comes as a blessed release from all that

threatens. It is strange that such a creed can have any
followers at all.

Strange indeed, I would say!

But now that he mentions a creed, let us examine his
attitudes to the articles of faith which we recite in the
creeds of the Church. It might be thought that belief in
'God the Father Almighty' was fairly safe – unless, of
course, one walks in the realms of the politically correct
who would prefer a choice between 'father' and 'mother'
and dislike anyway triumphalist words like 'almighty'.
Not so, for Hugh Dawes has theological objections,
which makes his argument rather more important. 'Divine
omnipotence,' he says, is 'a myth which no longer works
and now must honestly be let go of'. In fact, 'to talk
about God is quite simply to talk about life having
the capacity for meaning and purpose'. Does God exist
then as a being altogether different from the omnipo-
tent creator of biblical tradition? Or does he in fact
not exist in any sense in the way in which we have
understood?

He is clearer in his attitude to the doctrine of the incarnation, as three separate quotations will show. 'There is,'
he says, 'no longer any literal historical "incarnation" to
appeal to.' 'Though it is not history, and though Jesus was
a human being like the rest of us, [it] is valid myth.' 'His
purpose for us, his worth to us, is to show the possibilities
within us.'

I would agree that, yes, Jesus does show the possibilities
within us, but the Christian doctrine of the incarnation
is much more than that. He is also the means through
which, in St Paul's words, we can become 'filled with
all the fullness of God'. But that is not the same as
Dawes' interpretation where it becomes 'a progressive,
developing, living out of the God within us'. Is this New
Age pantheism? What it certainly is not is the Christian
doctrine of the incarnation.

Not surprisingly therefore, he rejects the bodily resurrection of Jesus, and indeed any understanding of the resurrection which might reasonably be equated with the New Testament revelation. He would, I think, dismiss this criticism, for he describes resurrection in these terms: 'Jesus' resurrection, we are saying, is to be most happily understood not as the promise of some sort of physical life beyond death *either for Jesus or for those who look to him* [emphasis added], but initially as the sense followers had of the vindication of the example of Jesus in that one life which, in common with the rest of us, was his.'

A number of biblical and credal understandings fall to the ground in that one paragraph: the resurrection of Christ, all the accounts of his resurrection appearances, all references to his continuing existence with the Father, his return in glory, his judgement of the world at the last day, and with it any possibility for us of 'the resurrection of the body and the life everlasting'.

For eternity has no place in 'open' Christianity: 'here and now is where we are all living, that surely is enough.' Not for me it isn't, nor for those to whom for nearly forty years I have ministered when they were approaching death themselves or were bereaved by the death of a loved one. Rather there is a sure and certain hope that 'whosoever liveth, and believeth in him, shall not die eternally.'[10] But for Hugh Dawes, 'Life beyond death has come to seem increasingly unlikely.' 'It does seem almost certain,' he says, 'that there will come a time when I am not, in terms of the self-awareness which makes me "me". This self will wholly cease to be.' 'Open believers are not deceived by myths of eternity.' No, that is quite clear!

That pretty well disposes of the creeds of the Church, or as Dawes puts it, 'the mock assurances of creeds and dogmas', 'the wooden assurances of conservative believers'. Little wonder that in turning his attention to the liturgy he can speak of the 'quite unwarranted weekly recital of a statement of fourth-century Christian beliefs, the Nicene Creed,' and declare that 'there is quite simply too much of the Bible in Christian worship at the present time.' The eucharist too, 'as with all of Christianity . . . is a human work'. I hope he can explain the point of worship. After all, 'when we pray,' he says, 'no one is listening outside ourselves.' It is 'a wholly human activity and none the worse for that'.

As for ethics, 'we must say straightforwardly that there just are not rules, in that old-fashioned sense of dictates from outside that are binding upon us.' He is dismissive of those who point to biblical moral standards: 'Some of these instructions are still frequently trotted out by Christian commentators as determinative for our actions and behaviour today.'

He uses the example of Christian opposition to abortion: 'So conservative Christians must manufacture support for their absolutist opposition to abortion, for instance, from traditions generated in the second century world and from general biblical positions on the sanctity of innocent life (an amalgam of biblical platitudes and emotional blackmail).'

So everything goes in open Christianity: doctrine, Bible, Christian ethics, salvation, eternal life. I do not question the integrity of Hugh Dawes's beliefs, nor do I suggest he does not have a profound faith, even if it is not recognisable as the Christian faith. I do not seek to hound him out of the Church, for it is his own conscience he must satisfy, not mine, that he can continue to hold a position and receive a salary. But I have to say that if I found that I shared his beliefs, I would resign my archdeaconry and spend my Sundays washing the car and mowing the lawn.[11]

I do not of course suggest that all 'liberal' (for want of a better description) Christians share all the views set out by Dawes. But one needs only read the Church press – not to mention the wilder events described on the national media – to know that to some degree these new theological understandings are beginning to permeate the life of the churches. The dismissal of the Revd Anthony Freeman by the Bishop of Chichester, Dr Eric Kemp, for denying the objective existence of God flushed out support from many clerical sympathisers. But there was no equally speedy support for Dr Kemp from his fellow bishops. It would be good to have episcopal assurance that a Christian is actually required to believe in God.

We do need a biblical faith, not unreasoned or unreasonable but compatible with scriptural revelation. We need to recognise sin, for this hurts the God we serve and the Jesus who is Love – and God – incarnate. Faith is belief and trust combined, and we need both: belief in the events which God prepared in order to bring us back to him, for to be with him is our entire purpose in creation; and we need to trust in the promises he has given to provide us on our journey with the strength and nourishment which is his divine grace. It is a return to the faith once delivered to the saints which will form the true basis for the good society from which we have so far strayed.

No one has put it more dramatically than St Paul:

That Christ may dwell in your hearts through faith; that you, being rooted and grounded in love, may have power to comprehend with all the saints what is the breadth and length and height and depth, and to know the love of Christ which passes knowledge, that you may be filled with all the fullness of God.[12]

7

Politics and Pulpit

Time's glory is to calm contending kings,
To unmask falsehood and bring truth to light.
Rape of Lucrece,1.939

'Politics and pulpit,' observed Edmund Burke, 'are terms
that have little agreement. No sound ought to be heard
in the church but the healing voice of Christian charity.'[1]
There are many who would say Amen to that, not least
when Church spokesmen challenge on Christian grounds
this or that article of political philosophy. They would
argue, with Burke, that 'surely the church is a place where
one day's truce ought to be allowed to the dissensions and
animosities of mankind'.[2]

And yet bishops sit in the House of Lords, and even
though the names now come from the Crown Appointments Commission, it is the Prime Minister who decides
which of the two names offered to him should be presented
to the Queen for nomination to a vacant see. When
the setting up of such a commission was considered
(in July 1976), suggestions were put forward that the
Church should present a name directly to the Crown
without the intervention of Downing Street. One of the
arguments used against this, at a press conference held by
the Prime Minister, was that it would be a constitutional
change giving power of election to the Lords, which was

the prerogative of the Crown only on the advice of the Prime Minister.

In other words, by presenting names to the Crown for nomination to a bishopric, the Prime Minister was *inter alia* nominating a future member of the House of Lords, which is a constitutional acknowledgment that politics and pulpit are not entirely separate and incompatible. If members of the bench of bishops can, by virtue of their office, become members of one of the Houses of Parliament, then that is a recognition that they have a contribution to make to the political life of the nation. Indeed it must surely therefore be the case that one of the considerations in their appointment must be their ability to contribute at this level.

There is no doubt that bishops do make a significant mark on the proceedings of the House of Lords, and their distinctive contribution here is in marked contrast to the reputation for general woolliness which they have gained for their leadership – or lack of it – in the national debate on the moral issues that disturb so many of their flock.

In particular in recent years, the debates which have taken place on highly technical and controversial government proposals in the field of education have seen important and highly praised contributions from successive chairmen of the General Synod Board of Education, first from the then Bishop of London, Dr Graham Leonard, and latterly from the recently retired Bishop of Guildford, Michael Adie.

The fact that they would receive considerable help from the staff of that board in the preparation of their speeches does not detract at all from the value of those contributions, since it differs only in source and not in kind from the assistance which a government minister would receive from his civil servants. There is, however, a potential danger here in episcopal contributions to the national debate, whether in the Lords, the General Synod or in wider Church or national arenas.

If a General Synod Board secretary or staff member who is asked to prepare such a speech or article is strongly committed to a party political stance, the lead which the Church delivers through its spokesman, episcopal or otherwise, may appear to be that of a politician rather than that of one who is distinctively a Christian. The Board for Social Responsibility fell deeply into this trap in earlier days, to be partly rescued with the appointment in 1976 of a strong chairman in Dr Graham Leonard (when Bishop of Truro). Even so, it was only with the arrival in 1982 of a new secretary, John Gladwin (now Bishop of Guildford), and latterly under the leadership of its present chairman, David Sheppard, Bishop of Liverpool, that the Board now appears to be on a more even keel and is happily far less suspect in its pronouncements than it was a decade ago.

The Church of England is often regarded as the Tory Party at prayer, though many Tories would now see it as the Far Left at prayer, and more than one Conservative Member of Parliament has expressed views similar (if couched more vociferously) to those of Edmund Burke, that 'no sound should be heard in church but the healing voice of Christian charity'. To heed such voices would be to deny Holy Scripture.

In the Old Testament, the prophet Isaiah rails against Israel as a 'sinful nation, a people laden with iniquity, offspring of evildoers, sons who deal corruptly! They have forsaken the Lord, they have despised the Holy One of Israel, they are utterly estranged.'[3]

Yet it is not that they have ceased to worship: the outward signs of faithfulness are there in the 'multitude of sacrifices' which they offer. But Isaiah tells them that the Lord cannot endure 'iniquity and solemn assembly' existing side by side: 'When you spread forth your hands, I will hide my eyes from you; even though you make many prayers, I will not listen.'[4]

Whatever the excellence and propriety of their worship, it is an outward sham if their devotion to the Lord is not also expressed in how they act towards others: 'Cease to do evil, learn to do good; seek justice, correct oppression; defend the fatherless, plead for the widow.'[5]

This is echoed later in Isaiah, who complains that the people only fast in order to quarrel and fight:

> Is not this the fact that I choose: to loose the bonds of wickedness, to undo the thongs of the yoke, to let the oppressed go free, and to break every yoke? Is it not to share your bread with the hungry, and bring the homeless into your house; when you see the naked, to cover him, and not to hide yourself from your own flesh?[6]

The same theme is taken up by the prophet Jeremiah:

> Thus says the Lord: Do justice and righteousness, and deliver from the hand of the oppressor him who has been robbed. And do no wrong or violence to the alien, the fatherless and the widow, nor shed innocent blood in this place.[7]

Jeremiah saw it as part of his call from God to enter the political field, or rather he saw no contradiction in translating his religious faith into social concern by proclaiming, as Shaftesbury was to do centuries later, that slaves should be released: 'that every one should set free his Hebrew slaves, male and female, so that no one should enslave a Jew, his brother.'[8]

Nehemiah took this further and ordered that interest on loans to fellow-Jews should cease to be exacted:

> I and my servants are lending them money and grain. Let us leave off this interest. Return to them this very day their fields, their vineyards, their olive orchards, and their houses, and the hundredth of money, grain, wine, and oil which you have been exacting of them.[9]

I was once explaining to an Orthodox Jewish rabbi the Anglican office book, the requirement that all clergy say daily from it morning and evening prayer, and how the old lectionary meant that over the course of a year, we read, roughly speaking, the whole of the Old Testament once and the New Testaments twice. 'Though we do leave out some of the more obscure legal passages in books like Deuteronomy and Leviticus,' I added. I found his reply salutary and not a little chastening: 'But we regard each verse of scripture to have equal importance with every other.'

A proper attitude to scripture then neither takes the commandments on morality – especially sexual morality – as paramount, leaving those which might be deemed to be 'political' as of a secondary importance; nor does it emphasise the collective duty to the poor or disadvantaged or any other group while ignoring the need to observe a personal morality. It is easy to fall into either fault, as today's Church shows only too clearly.

The New Testament is equally firm in its teaching. For St James, we are to be 'doers of the word and not hearers only', displaying a faith which leads us both to personal holiness as well as to concern for those less fortunate.

If any one thinks he is religious, and does not bridle his tongue but deceives his heart, this man's religion is vain. Religion that is pure and undefiled before God and the Father is this: to visit orphans and widows in their affliction, and to keep oneself unstained from the world.[10]

The message could hardly be clearer.

James demands that we show no partiality because of a person's station in life, in a timely warning for today's vicar or churchwarden:

For a man with gold rings and in fine clothing comes into

your assembly, and a poor man in shabby clothing also comes in, and you pay attention to the one who wears the fine clothing and say, 'Have a seat here, please,' while you say to the poor man, 'Stand there,' or 'Sit at my feet,' have you not made distinctions among yourselves, and become judges with evil thoughts?[11]

St John's message is the same:

But if any one has the world's goods and sees his brother in need, yet closes his heart against him, how does God's love abide in him? Little children, let us not love in word or speech but in deed and in truth.[12]

The same meaning comes clearly through the teaching of Jesus himself in his parable of the rich man and Lazarus:

a rich man, who was clothed in purple and fine linen and who feasted sumptuously every day. And at his gate lay a poor man named Lazarus, full of sores, who desired to be fed with what fell from the rich man's table; moreover the dogs came and licked his sores.[13]

When the rich man died, because he did nothing for Lazarus, he would suffer in eternal separation from God, whereas Lazarus would be in 'Abraham's bosom'.

Some suggest that the characters in the stories told by Jesus were in some cases based on real people known to his hearers. But without that added personal touch, the situations were sufficiently common to be identifiable, perhaps uncomfortably so, to those to whom they were related.

When Jesus declares to the 'unrighteous' at his left hand:

'Depart from me, you cursed, into the eternal fire prepared for the devil and his angels; for I was hungry and you gave me no food, I was thirsty and you gave me no drink. I was a stranger and you did not welcome me, naked and you did not clothe me, sick and in prison and you did not visit me.'[14]

When, they ask in desperation, did we not do these things?

Then he will answer them, 'Truly, I say to you, as you did it not to one of the least of these, you did it not to me.'[15]

Jesus himself is fierce in his condemnation of the scribes and Pharisees, and one wonders what the reaction would be if a modern-day bishop (or archdeacon, perish the thought) used such language:

'Woe to you, scribes and Pharisees, hypocrites! for you tithe mint and dill and cumin, and have neglected the weightier matters of the law, justice and mercy and faith; these you ought to have done *without neglecting the others* [emphasis added].[16]

It is important to recognise that Jesus does not give a choice between worship, justice and faith: each is as important as the other, for the sake of the wholeness of a spiritual human being, and we neglect any at our peril.

There is indeed no part of life which can be said to have no religious implications: relationships, the family, war and peace, home and foreign affairs, unemployment, homelessness, poverty, health care, or whatever.

Thus the bishop or other Church leader who dips his toe into such issues in his sermons or writing is in no way venturing outside his remit, and on the contrary to ignore them is to neglect part of the Lord's commission. It is the government minister or back-bench Member of Parliament who in criticising such comment, deserves condemnation for failing himself to put religious faith above party political commitment.

Unfortunately the 'political' bishop can fall into the same trap, and political involvement by Church leaders in recent years has not been by any means pure and unsullied. Just as there is a biblical imperative to apply one's Christian faith to every corner of daily existence, so there is an equally strict commitment to put the demands of God before those of the secular world. The cry of the 1960s, that the world should write the Church's agenda, is false and dangerously misleading: only God can give the Church its agenda.

In his final commission to his followers, Jesus told them:

> 'If the world hates you, know that it has hated me before it hated you. If you were of the world, the world would love its own; but because you are not of the world, but I chose you out of the world, therefore the world hates you.'[17]

St James has no doubt that God comes first:

> Unfaithful creatures! Do you not know that friendship with the world is enmity with God? Therefore whoever wishes to be a friend of the world makes himself an enemy of God.[18]

It is to the shame of the Church that in the decades since the 1960s, the desperate quest to be relevant and credible in a world increasingly hostile to Christian values has led to a friendship with the world and a consequent 'enmity with God'. This was nowhere more true than in its involvement with the situation in southern Africa. Racism, especially in its statutory embodiment in the evil doctrine of *apartheid*, demanded a Christian response. In the words of the prophet Isaiah, believers are to 'seek justice, to correct oppression',[19] and for the Church to have closed its eyes to the vicious evil of *apartheid* would have been totally to betray that trust and command.

That South Africa now has an elected multi-racial government and a black President was a victory for brave men and women who gave their lives and liberty in opposing *apartheid* within South Africa. But credit must also go to those outside the country whose pressure gave courage to their protests and at the same time helped to change the consciences of politicians and people alike.

But that does not mean that wrong things were not done in the name of justice and in the fight against oppression. I had lunch one day in South Africa with a black Anglican priest who worked amongst the poorest of the poor in a squatter camp. He had been a member of the African National Congress over many years, and had suffered beatings and imprisonment at the hands of the authorities.

'But now,' he told me, 'I am unpopular with both sides. For now I tell the ANC that it is as wrong for the ANC to kill a white policeman as it is for a white policeman to kill the ANC.' Could he be in serious trouble for this? I asked. He smiled and replied quietly, 'My life is in danger.' It is this kind of witness which is the true political contribution of the Christian, of the sort which says in effect, through the words of St Paul, 'I will show you a still more excellent way.'[20] Unfortunately the Church has sometimes shown that it prefers the less excellent but easier path of the party politician.

One of the longest running sagas in Church debate in the years since 1970 has been the conflict of opinion on the World Council of Churches' political involvement, particularly in relation to the so-called 'liberation movements' then active in southern Africa, and the grants allocated to them by the WCC's Programme to Combat Racism. It was characteristic that it was to the Marxist rather than to the moderate groups that the WCC chose to make its largest allocations. Yet atrocities as ugly as those perpetrated by the forces of the white regimes had been committed by those same liberation movements, causing outrage among many church folk in Britain.

In a debate in the General Synod in 1978, I proposed an amendment which asked for an inquiry into the issues raised through the WCC's action and not least into the 'theological basis for our continued membership of the WCC'. I had been privately encouraged and supported in this by a number of bishops, and it was my first experience of the fear of putting private concern into public voice.

I was of course accused of racism and the bishops feared the same criticism, as did other clergy members in Synod, who rightly recognised that it would do their personal careers no good at all. It was also my first experience in the General Synod (though by no means the first in the British Council of Churches Assembly) of the techniques used by clever debaters in damaging the cause of an opponent.

I had made it clear that atrocities on either side were to be condemned, and that we ought to continue our membership of the World Council of Churches. The most powerful speech against my amendment came from a well-known contributor on political issues, Canon Paul Oestreicher, a power in the land in those far-off days and a formidable polemicist.

Oestreicher told the Synod, careful not to mention my name, that

it would be rank hypocrisy of Synod, stirred by the emotions of people in our Church who are deeply troubled by the atrocities on one side and not troubled by the atrocities on the other, it would be profound hypocrisy for us to stand up and lecture the World Council of Churches.[21]

Having sowed that seed in the middle of his contribution, he ended with a direct attack on my speech:

Consider what the world beyond these shores would think if this little Church of England were even going to discuss what Mr Austin had asked us to discuss – the implications of leaving the World Council. The very impression of that would be of a self-righteous and unrealistic Church of England.[22]

The fact that I had condemned atrocities by whomsoever they were committed and had called for a stronger involvement in the work of the Council was lost behind the clever distortions and the use of pejorative phrases such as 'profound hypocrisy', 'self-righteous and unrealistic'. I record it here simply because it happened to me, and I remember the helpless frustration at being unable to counter it with the truth. But it is a technique which has been used again and again by many in Synod debates on politically sensitive issues, to the great discredit of a Christian debating chamber.

But 1978 is a long time ago, and the issues under debate are consigned to history. Yet they do recall a more recent case of political involvement by the churches. In the course of my own speech in that debate, I made reference to SWAPO, the South-West Africa People's Organisation, 'whose Communist leadership, in its pursuit of democratic justice for all in free Namibia, *imprisoned without trial in Tanzania those black moderates who wished to enter into discussion with the other non-white political groups in that country*' (emphasis added).[23]

These injustices were well known in international church circles, including those in the Church of England concerned in these areas, though they only came to more public notice in 1989, when Namibia became free, and the detainees returned home. Even a delegation from the Anglican Communion with members totally committed both to liberation and to SWAPO as the legitimate representatives of the people of that country commented in their Report:

We are aware too, that there have been incidents of denial of human rights and the use of torture among and within groups struggling for liberation. Where it has occurred it needs to be acknowledged and those responsible held accountable.[24]

Only the Lutheran World Federation comes out of this sorry tale with its integrity intact. An LWF press release of October 1989 is a model of Christian involvement in the political process, and for that reason I reproduce it in full:

The Lutheran World Federation is shocked and dismayed by reports of torture and killing of prisoners by personnel of SWAPO, according to LWF general secretary, Dr Gunnar Staalsett. The allegations of violence were made recently by former prisoners of SWAPO who were released by the liberation movement under the terms of an amnesty that is part of Namibia's independence process. While South Africa had infiltrated some of SWAPO's refugee camps in Angola and Zambia, Staalsett said, 'This in no way excuses the behaviour of some SWAPO personnel as described in the recent reports.'

In an oral statement to journalists here [in Geneva], Staalsett said that the LWF is committed to protesting the violation of human rights 'on an even-handed basis.' Following a discussion on Namibia the LWF Executive Committee voted in August 'to reaffirm its insistence on due process and humane treatment for all detainees and prisoners and, therefore, categorically deplores any action by any party concerned which is in violation of such principles.'

The LWF has never identified itself totally with any liberation movement, but has relationships on an *ad hoc* basis, Staalsett said. 'There are points at which our interests coincide, that is for the liberation of oppressed people, but there are also points at which we are not identical, that is in ways and means to achieve liberation. At times there is convergence and at times there is a great discrepancy between us,' he added.

The treatment of prisoners in SWAPO camps has been the subject of frequent discussion between the LWF and SWAPO, the general secretary said. The most recent letter on this subject dates from June 1988 and included documentation based on information provided by the Parents' Committee that has claimed to represent the SWAPO prisoners. 'We are the only international organisation that has taken these accusations so seriously that we are willing to risk sending a delegation to Angola to try to come a little closer to the matter,' said Staalsett.[25]

It is sad that other Christian bodies at home and abroad did not follow the same model in their political involvement on this and other issues. As late as 1991 when I was preparing to go to Australia as a delegate to the wcc Canberra Assembly, I was taken aside by a staff member of the General Synod to be told, 'We hope no one is going to raise the matter of the treatment of SWAPO detainees during the Assembly.'

But the General Synod's involvement in this area surely reached its nadir in a debate in July 1986 when it considered a report on South Africa by the Board for Social Responsibility. The debate took place against a background of violence in South Africa, perpetrated by the security forces on the one hand and radical elements of the African National Congress on the other. In full view of international television teams, police action in the townships was brutal, deliberate and indiscriminate, and one can only assume that where the press were not present, the repression was even worse.

But ANC violence was no less brutal, and beatings and executions were proliferating, some by the terrible method of 'necklacing', while bombs were placed in stores and at bus stops, causing death and injury to victims of all races. There could hardly have been a more propitious time for the Church to make a Christian comment on a political issue, nor a more proper occasion to speak up against oppression and injustice.

I proposed an amendment deploring the 'indiscriminate use of terror and violence against innocent men, women and children, whether perpetrated by the African National Congress or the South African Government'. Archbishop Desmond Tutu had made a similar plea in South Africa, and it seemed a modest and appropriate comment to make in the circumstances. It did not deny the ANC members' right to defend themselves; nor did it suggest that the government forces had no duty to contain violence when attacked.

It was similar to the kind of response, balanced in its criticism and condemnation, made by the churches in Northern Ireland out of their own pain at the effects of violence from the Provisional IRA and other nationalist terrorist groups on the one hand and from so-called Loyalist paramilitaries on the other. Its content was – to me at any rate – so obviously the sort of political intervention Christians have a duty to make that I foolishly imagined it would be accepted without question.

That was, to say the least, naïve of someone as well aware of the political predilections of Church bodies as I have become over the years. The official response which came was the most chilling contribution I have ever heard on the subject, and was delivered by a kind and gentle bishop, Simon Barrington-Ward of Coventry. Its content was so contrary to everything I know of him that I can only assume he was delivering a speech prepared for him by others. In it he said:

Of course we all deplore violence and the kind of terrorist acts that have been mentioned. But at the same time

I think that my reluctance to accept this amendment is rooted in the kind of lofty even-handedness towards the ANC on the one hand and to the Government on the other which it implies. When we realise that the ANC struggled for a long time by peaceful means and has been rooted in a peaceful approach, and only gradually came to the idea of any act of violence being used, because of the way in which their people were being treated and they themselves were being arrested, one might have commended the loftier, Gandhian path of passive resistance, but it is very difficult, unless you are really in the heart of it yourself and struggling with it. Anything they have done is tiny in comparison with the enormous machine and power of state violence that is there and is imposed all the time and which creates the situation out of which their acts have arisen.[26]

Leaving aside the fact that I had not called for a 'loftier, Ghandian path of passive resistance' but for a condemnation of 'the indiscriminate use of terror and violence against innocent men, women and children, whether perpetrated by the African National Congress or the South African government', the Bishop of Coventry's speech was effectively an absolution pronounced on any group – in South Africa or elsewhere – which might excuse its indiscriminate actions in planting bombs or indulging in mass shootings on the grounds that their group was 'rooted in a peaceful approach, and only gradually came to the idea of any act of violence being used, because of the way in which their people were being treated'. I was sickened by it and wondered what kind of Church I was serving.

It is this kind of response, common to a wide variety of political issues in which the Church has become involved, which has given the impression that the Church of England is the Militant Tendency at prayer. The fact that it is sometimes a perfectly justifiable impression can obscure the other side of the coin. For the Church, both through its bishops and through the General Synod, has made appropriate and valuable political contributions on many current social and political problems.

The much-criticised report, *Faith in the City*, though at first condemned out-of-hand by government spokesmen as a 'left-wing' analysis, proved to be a catalyst for change in the living conditions of society in the deprived areas of our inner cities. If the Church has no view on such matters as unemployment, redundancy, educational policy, the family, child abuse, pornography, Sunday trading, health care – to name only a few – then it fails to enter the life of the people it seeks to serve, and its faith becomes only other-worldly.

A church which claims an incarnate God in Jesus Christ, a God who entered his created world uniquely and intentionally, must have a faith which relates to the world into which he entered and took flesh.

If it does not, then Karl Marx was right to denounce religion as 'the opium of the people'[27] and Charles Kingsley to say: 'We have used the Bible as if it was a constable's handbook – an opium dose for keeping beasts of burden patient while they are being overloaded.'[28]

Always the Church must keep close hold of St Paul's injunction, if its contribution in the political arena is to be Christian and theological rather than secular and politically partisan:

> Do not be conformed to this world but be transformed by the renewal of your mind, that you may prove what is the will of God, what is good and acceptable and perfect.[29]

The tragedy comes where the Church has allowed the world to write its agenda, facing the world's problems and injustices with its mind untransformed by God's renewing insights but conformed only to the inadequate answers of a sinful society.

8

A Church Established

Though this be madness, yet there is method in it.
Hamlet, ii.ii.211

Starting with a clean slate, there could be no justification for the creation of an established Church of England. It would be unthinkable that a religious body, founded to maintain and promote the teachings of Jesus Christ, would demand a special status in the land such as establishment gives to the Church of England.

The Church could not defend the automatic presence of the Archbishops of Canterbury and York, the Bishops of London, Durham and Winchester and twenty-one other bishops as members of the House of Lords, nor that many should live in castles and palaces in recognition of a former secular power.

It could not assume that the monarch be its Supreme Governor, nor that he or she at the coronation should promise to maintain the 'Protestant Reformed religion'. It could not claim the right to minister to the whole population of England, nor a privileged position in the promulgation of ecclesiastical law. In short, to create the establishment of the Church of England from nothing would mean an assumption of privilege totally in conflict with the principles which it was intended as a church to promote.

But we do not start from scratch. Establishment is a fact, and a case must be made for its retention, its amendment, or its removal. It is popularly said, sometimes by those who ought to know better, that the Church of England owes its origin to the political and marital problems of Henry VIII, which would make nonsense of Archbishop Carey's rightful claim to be the 103rd Archbishop of Canterbury, in a direct and unbroken line from Augustine who landed in Kent in AD 597. And for that matter, of my own claim to the 80th Archdeacon of York in 902 years from Archdeacon Durand in the year 1093.

Indeed, *Anglicana Ecclesia*, the Church of England, traces its origins to a date even before the arrival of St Augustine, and had always seen much tension in its ties with Rome and the Papacy, long before the theological and political conflicts which came to a head during the reign of Tudor monarchs.

The variety of doctrinal influences which shaped the theology of the post-Reformation Church are not, however, the issue here, but rather the relations between Church and State which led to the present establishment of the Church of England. Two Acts of Parliament could be said to have formed the twin pillars of that post-Reformation Church of England, the Acts of Supremacy and Uniformity. We must also consider the submission of clergy and the appropriation by Henry VIII of ecclesiastical revenues, as well as the manner of appointment of bishops and other dignitaries (which will be the subject of a separate chapter), all of which have their effect on the present establishment of the Church of England as they do on the case for and against disestablishment.

Indeed, the rationale for disestablishment can fall into confusion when the differing strands are not separated, for although all are to some extent interconnected, the force of argument for and against is not equally distributed.

The first Act of Uniformity was passed in 1549, giving sole authority to the 1549 Book of Common Prayer and laying severe penalties on those clergy who failed to use it, with lesser penalties for the laity who might speak against the said Book. It was revised in an Act of 1552, again in 1559, and yet again in 1662 after the Restoration. Additionally in the latter, all ministers and schoolmasters were required to make a declaration against taking up arms against the king. Quite apart from its political elements, the Act of Uniformity sought to bring a uniformity of worship to the Church of England.

In the words of the Preface to the 1662 Book of Common Prayer:

> And whereas heretofore there hath been great diversity in saying and singing in Churches within this Realm; some following Salisbury Use, some Hereford Use, and some the Use of Bangor, some of York, some of Lincoln; now from henceforth all the whole Realm shall have but one Use.

It must be remembered too that *lex orandi, lex credendi* (what we pray is what we believe) is an important principle of Anglican life, and in seeking uniformity of worship at a time of theological turmoil, there was the worthy motive of ensuring that what was said within worship conformed to the official teaching of the Church. The Act of Uniformity was only repealed in 1974 as one of the provisions of the Church of England (Worship and Doctrine) Measure of that year.

On 7 November 1972 at the General Synod, Archbishop Michael Ramsey introduced a report, 'Church and State – Worship and Doctrine', in the course of which he said:

> Two things seem certain. It seems certain that there is a general wish within the Church that the partnership between Church and State should continue; at least we have no proposal before us for the ending of that partnership. It also seems certain that there is a general

wish within the Church that the Church as represented in the General Synod should be the body which controls the Church's doctrine and worship.[1]

He went on to quote from Archbishop Davidson's statement, made in July 1928 on behalf of the entire episcopate of the two Provinces of York and Canterbury, when Davidson said:

It is a fundamental principle that the Church, that is, the bishops together with the clergy and laity, must in the last resort, when its mind has been fully ascertained, retain its inalienable right, in loyalty to our Lord and Saviour Jesus Christ, to formulate its faith in Him and to arrange the expression of that Holy Faith in its form of worship.[2]

Ramsey went on to make a comparison with the Scottish Kirk, also established but with much greater freedom, and argued that:

It is quite impossible to expect the State to have an exclusive partnership with a Church which might turn itself into any sort of Church at will, say, Calvinist or Lutheran or Papist . . . The liberty of the Scottish Kirk is linked with clearly spelt out definitions of its identity so long as its link with the State continues.[3]

Supporting the Archbishop of Canterbury, the Bishop of London, Dr Gerald Ellison, underlined the reference to:

the established Church which possesses this freedom (to order its worship and doctrine), and has protected the essential character of the Kirk and I am sure we shall always retain the essential quality of the Church of England.[4]

Ellison insisted that

> We recognise that, in view of the special relationship between Church and State, the State is entitled to guarantees that the General Synod will not depart from its traditional character in such a way as to disqualify the Church of England from its privileged position.[5]

In fact, the effect of the Worship and Doctrine Measure (of 1974) in the twenty years of its operation has been to produce a plethora of worship books, well-intended and certainly meeting the needs of many worshippers, but which has tended to move Anglican worship away from any concept of uniformity. Moreover, there are many, not least within the General Synod, who would wish to dispense with the catholic and sacramental elements of the Church which were preserved in the Reformation settlement, while preserving the essentials of the faith as revealed in Holy Scripture.

Alongside them, but in total disagreement, are others who see the provisions of the Worship and Doctrine Measure as a freedom to abandon traditional doctrines firmly based in scripture, towards a radical reassessment of Christianity which would bear little comparison with the faith of the Church of England as set down in its formularies.

Disestablishment would mean that those who wish to break faith with the assurances given to Parliament at the time of the passing of the Worship and Doctrine Measure would be given almost unlimited powers to change the Church of England. Even now, a lawyer, a senior member of the General Synod, has said, 'If the General Synod declares that Jesus Christ did not rise from the dead, then that is the doctrine of the Church of England.'

Notwithstanding the provisions of the Worship and

Doctrine Measure and the interpretation of one lawyer, and even without the Act of Uniformity, establishment does give some safeguards against the hijacking of the Church by those wedded to strange doctrines.

The Act of Supremacy of 1534 confirmed to King Henry VIII and his successors the title of 'only supreme head in earth of the Church of England, called *Anglicana Ecclesia*'. It marked the end (for a time) of a bitter conflict between monarch and Church, partly concerned with power of the Church in respect of ecclesiastical law, partly with Henry's desire to find a wife who might produce a male heir, but especially with privileges of Rome and – as the King perceived it – the dangerous double loyalty of the Church, on the one hand to himself as monarch and on the other to the Papacy.

The anti-Papal character of Henry's Act of Supremacy inevitably meant that it would be repealed by the Catholic Queen Mary, and that repeal was confirmed by Elizabeth I. However in the first Act of her reign, Elizabeth produced a new Act of Supremacy by which she was declared, not 'the *only supreme head in earth* of the Church of England' of Henry's Act, but 'the *only supreme governor* of this, and of all other her highness's dominions and countries, as well in all spiritual or ecclesiastical things or causes as temporal' (emphasis added).

There are differing assessments of the attitude of the general public to these matters.

While, therefore, it is true to say that the vast bulk of the nation were untouched by any desire to revolt from the old faith, it is equally true to affirm that they were not moved by any marked desire to defend it. The whole dispute about England's relations to Rome was beyond the lay mind.[6]

Although the strongest opposition to change was to be found in the conservative House of Lords, nevertheless the forces of the old order were depleted, with no less than ten sees vacant, and the abbots no longer there through the dissolution of the monasteries. The clergy were the only organised body capable of making a reasoned opposition, but they were given no opportunity to influence events: even Convocation was deliberately ignored.

In March of 1559 a debate was staged in Westminster Hall, but it was not intended that this should be a free discussion. Because those of the catholic party, who claimed they had not been properly informed of the arrangements, refused to abide by the conditions laid down for the debate, two of their leaders, Bishops White of Winchester and Watson of Lincoln, were sent to the Tower and the remainder heavily fined – hardly an encouragement to open debate.

The concept of royal supremacy had its origins in the principle of the divine right of kings which few today would defend. Queen Elizabeth I understood the powers with which she was invested by the Act of Supremacy to be greater than the gloss put down upon them by the government, supposedly to make it more acceptable to the catholic party, which resented any idea of a regal supremacy by a lay person over the Church.

Certainly 'it did transfer, as the subsequent publication of royal Injunctions clearly shows, the right to make ordinances touching spiritual matters. Some of the queen's counsellors went so far as to maintain that she had power under the law equal to that of the Pope or Archbishop of Canterbury, extending even to the articles of faith.'[7]

It is hard indeed to justify the Act of Supremacy today, given its history and the unacceptable assumptions which its existence implies. At the same time, there is a strong argument for the head of state to be also the leading member of a national church, with responsibilities to every citizen. The Church of England is also a folk church, that is to say that for some it is the church to which they feel they belong but which they rarely attend, save for the rites of passage such as baptism, marriage and burial. Such a concept can be criticised by those who desire a tidier and more committed membership. But others recognise it as a valid if residual acknowledgment of a spiritual dimension to life, and many clergy in ministering to that dimension would greatly regret its inevitable disappearance if disestablishment were to come.

On 11 May 1532, the King sent for the Speaker and a dozen Members of Parliament to tell them that he had discovered that the clergy 'of our realm be but half our subjects, yea and scarce our subjects'. As proof of this assertion, he produced copies of the oath which prelates made to the Pope on their consecration, and demanded that it be read in Parliament.

This threat brought to heel a rebellious Convocation on 15 May 1532, in what came to be known as the submission of the clergy. By its terms, Convocation promised to

> make no new constitutions, canons or ordinances without the royal licence; the existing body of ecclesiastical law must be reviewed by a committee of thirty-two, half-clerical, half-lay, all chosen by the king; the laws approved by the majority of the committee must receive the royal assent before they became valid.[8]

This is not far from the present requirement that Measures passed by the General Synod must be considered by the Ecclesiastical Committee of members of both Houses of Parliament. If a majority declare the Measure to be 'expedient', it is then laid before Parliament which can accept it or reject it but not amend it. It becomes law only when it has received the Royal Assent. Some see this as an unwarranted interference by the State in Church affairs. But it does give a freedom to pass legislation for which in certain matters other churches might have to seek an Act of Parliament.

Elizabeth's Act of Supremacy went much further than

that of Henry VIII. The election of bishops by *congé d'élire* (see p. 90) was restored, and an oath of obedience to the Crown was imposed in all things ecclesiastical as well as civil. It was made compulsory for all clergy, judges, justices, mayors, any persons taking holy orders or receiving degrees at universities. Refusal led to loss of office, and anyone attempting to maintain the authority of 'a foreign prince, prelate or potentate' (with the Pope unmentioned but intended) would, on the third offence, be liable to death for high treason.

In those days the bishops were men of principle, and with one exception (Kitchen of Llandaff) all refused to have anything to do with either the oath of supremacy or the prayer book. It placed the government in a dilemma since to make martyrs of almost the entire bench would hardly have been politically wise. 'Some were detained in a condition of semi-imprisonment in the custody of the new state bishops who took their place; others were given their liberty conditionally.'⁹ Of the rest, eight were sent to the Tower and the elderly York and Durham allowed to retire to their country estates.

The courage and unanimity of the bishops was in no way matched by a similar attention to conscience among the lower ranks of the clergy, and their abject surrender to the government was described even by catholic commentators as a *débâcle*. It is impossible to judge the actual numbers, but what is clear is that the vast majority of clergy who happily served under the Catholic Queen Mary passed over into the service of new establishment without a murmur. 'But the loyalty of the priests who took the oath was often qualified by time-serving, and watchful readiness to revive the past whenever fortune's wheel should take another turn.'¹⁰ The oath of obedience is of course still required today, on ordination, on consecration as bishop, and by an incumbent on taking office. With the New Testament in the right hand, the new minister will say, 'I, *A B*, do swear that I will be faithful and bear true allegiance to Her Majesty Queen Elizabeth II, her heirs and successors, according to law: So help me God.'

Even convinced anti-disestablishmentarians can question the need for this requirement in the twentieth century, without embracing the arguments for disestablishment. It is a child of its age, anti-Papal from a time when to support the Papal claims was to own allegiance to a foreign potentate. It was a requirement laid upon the clergy whereby they would declare before God their secular as well as their ecclesiastical loyalty. It is irrelevant today and not a little offensive.

The effect of the submission of clergy was to make the king supreme in all ecclesiastical causes, and two years later it was incorporated in an Act of Parliament, which coupled with it restraint of appeals to Rome. As Henry struggled with the English clergy, so he began his assault on the privileges of Rome. It was a requirement that annates, the first year's revenue of an ecclesiastical benefice, be paid to the Papal curia, and this was reduced in 1532 to only 5 per cent of the net revenue of any benefice.

Conditionally restrained in this way in 1532, the payment of annates was transferred to the Crown in 1534 under the Annates Statute, and finally converted into 'Queen Anne's Bounty' in 1704. In 1948, the Ecclesiastical Commissioners and Queen Anne's Bounty were combined to form the Church Commissioners for England, to manage the estates and revenues of the Church of England.

The Church Commissioners report to the General Synod but are responsible to Parliament. Recent revelations have shown that there have been insufficient safeguards, particularly with regard to investment policy and accountability. Its Assets Committee, for example, was protected by statute from being answerable even to the Commissioners' Board of Governors.

Changes will be made, but it would be a mistaken reform if, with the principles of disestablishment in mind, the Commissioners were to be made accountable to the General Synod. An increasing proportion of the Commissioners' income provides for pensions for retired clergy, and the Maxwell affair has shown that pension funds need all the defence they can acquire. Already there have been attempts by less responsible elements within the General Synod to divert Commissioners' funds into other objects.

But Parliament can safeguard the rights of the intended recipients of Commissioners' income, and even in a disestablished Church, that involvement should continue. The spectre of disendowment as a possible result of disestablishment can be dismissed: no government dare emulate Robert Maxwell's plundering of the Mirror Group pension fund.

We have examined four of the five strands of the establishment of the Church of England (apart from the matter of the appointment of bishops which has a chapter to itself), each with differing contributions to, and importance within, the arguments for and against disestablishment.

It was made clear by Archbishop Michael Ramsey that the Worship and Doctrine Measure of 1974 was not intended as a move towards disestablishment, even though it involved the repeal of the Act of Uniformity of 1662. But nor was it to be an undermining of the Reformation settlement which shaped the theological position of the Church of England. Indeed the Bishop of London, Dr Gerald Ellison, was at pains to recognise that 'the State is entitled to guarantees that the General Synod will not depart from its traditional character in such a way as to disqualify the Church of England from its privileged position'.[11]

The right kind of privilege – and in fact the only kind which Church leaders ought to seek to preserve – is one which demands duties and service, rather than 'the best seats in the synagogue'.[12] And the 'privileged position' of the Church of England as a national church by law established is one which gives it the responsibility of ministering, if required, to every citizen, without qualification. The Church needs the residual involvement with the State in order to preserve that duty against the iconoclastic tendencies of the General Synod. With disestablishment, it could be in grave danger.

In the same way, there is little justification for the requirement that clergy take an oath of allegiance to the monarch, nor for the monarch continuing to hold the title of 'Supreme Governor', since the political purpose of each has become an historical irrelevance. Nevertheless, for the monarch to be the chief lay person of the national church is an important symbolic reminder that, in a just society, secular and spiritual are inextricably linked. Of course to abandon the solemnity of the formal title of the monarch would not reduce the representative demands on that person but rather would deepen them. It would be a greater anomaly for an admitted and unreformed adulterer (let us say – hypothetically, of course) to be Chief Lay Person in a national church than it would be for him to be an impersonal and formal Supreme Governor.

In a similar way, the removal of the Lords Spiritual from Parliament would give a signal that society (through the State) had now no need of such an influence in the deliberations of Parliament. Yet at the same time to confine the Lords Spiritual to bishops of the Church of England cannot be defended in our ecumenical and multi-faith society. Reform of this would come with disestablishment, and ought to come without it.

The Church Commissioners, it has been argued, should remain answerable to Parliament, again as a safeguard against the General Synod and to preserve the pension rights of those who have served the Church. So disestablishment need not mean disendowment, nor the abandonment of this parliamentary duty.

With or without disestablishment, anomalies and abuses can be remedied, and it is a misuse of debate to argue for one course or another when this is so, as it is when the end result – as in the appointment of bishops and other dignitaries – remains unchanged. Nor is it an argument against the principle of disestablishment to warn of the danger of giving too much power to the General Synod.

At the heart of the argument against disestablishment is the understanding that sacred and secular are linked, that there needs to be the acknowledgment that the establishment of the Church brings different and important insights into national debate. It indicates to both church and state that there is a higher authority than human desire and the limits of human reason, which must be consulted in the political search for a just and ordered society, a 'still more excellent way'[13] that will help transform flawed secular society into the City of God. By an accident of history, it is for us the Church of England which is by law established. We would have been wrong to choose it as a privilege, but we should be ignoring the duty God has laid upon us if we abandoned it.

9

By Appointment Only

I am a feather for each wind that blows.
The Winter's Tale, II.iii.153

The Oxford Dictionary of the Christian Church records that

> according to the Chronicle of Ingulphus of Crowland, a contemporary of William the Conqueror, the disposal of English sees had already been for some centuries in the hand of the English Kings. Disputes with the Popes about this royal prerogative arose under William Rufus. In 1214 King John agreed that bishops should be elected by the dean and chapter of the cathedral, but that the royal permission to proceed to the election, the *congé d'élire*, must first be secured, and the election to be confirmed by Royal Assent afterwards.[1]

Certainly there had been problems in the previous century, not least in York. In 1143, William Fitzherbert, Treasurer of York Minster and a king's chaplain, was consecrated Archbishop of York as nominee, in effect, of the king, much to the fury of the monks and not least of the Archdeacon of York, Osbert de Baines. On William's nomination to the see, Osbert had headed the dissidents of the chapter and appealed to Rome, on the grounds that William was no more than the King's pawn and that there were irregularities in his election.

King Stephen responded by imprisoning the archdeacon (as no doubt other royals would have wished to do in later years – the prison was Byrham Castle in Lincolnshire, in case Christopher Soames should be interested). Unfortunately for William, Eugenius III became Pope and as a fellow-member (with some of the major opponents) of the Cistercian order was more sympathetic to the objectors. William was deposed, and remained in refuge in Winchester, living in simplicity, praying and studying, and gaining a reputation for sanctity.

The death of his most prominent enemies and the election of a more sympathetic pope led to William's return to York in 1154, where he died in suspicious circumstances a few months later. The 'suspicious circumstances' led to a charge being laid against Archdeacon Osbert that he had served a poisoned chalice to the archbishop at mass. Osbert naturally denied the charge, which was never finally proven, though the denial failed to carry conviction and Osbert was unfrocked. Meanwhile William was eventually canonised as St William of York.

Such clashes between Church and State, as well as between Church and Pope, were by no means uncommon. When in 1534 the Annates Statute was passed, in case of Papal retaliation against the restraint of annates or if for example the Pope would not issue the necessary Bull approving a bishop's appointment, it was enacted that a bishop sould be consecrated by the archbishop of his province and an archbishop by a commission of two bishops appointed by the king. It was in effect a declaration of independence, and ensured the present system of appointment of bishops by the Crown.

It is likely, given human nature, that no system of episcopal appointment would be without its pitfalls, and it is some evidence of divine influence, however remote and indirect, that good bishops have emerged from time to time throughout the history of the Church of England.

In the early eighteenth century, there were men like Burnet of Salisbury, Sharp of York, Wake of Lincoln and later Canterbury, and Gibson, first of Lincoln and then of London. Even so, it was unlikely that any clergyman who did not support – indeed, did not devote himself to promoting – the Whig interest would ever be thought suitable for episcopal or any other preferment. The system clearly was open to corruption and sycophancy.

Moorman records:

Clergy who were ambitious, as indeed most of them were, knew how to play their cards and obtain preferment. He who had the good fortune to have been born a member of one of the noble families began well ahead of his less privileged rivals. Against the man who had no such good luck the dice were heavily loaded; but by skill and fortune he might get into the graces of some aristocratic family, perhaps as a successful tutor or chaplain, and so win their support. The next thing was to preach the right kind of sermons, publish the right kind of pamphlets and do good work for your party in parish and county, the rest followed in due course.[2]

For more than one bishop, who hoped for promotion to a better endowed diocese, and needed to spend time in London, especially in the House of Lords where he could meet the right people and make the right noises, the pastoral care of the flock committed to his charge was of little concern. Hoadly was Bishop of Bangor for six years and Bishop of Hereford for the next two, and never set foot in either diocese.

Governmental patrons naturally expected a political return on their patronage and were rarely disappointed. At the time of the Jacobite risings of 1715 and 1745,

Nicolson of Carlisle and Herring of York organised resistance within their dioceses, raising funds, reviewing troops and even calling men to arms. At elections, bishops would bring pressure to bear on clergy to vote for Whig candidates, and with such an example of political conformity from their father-in-God, it was hardly surprising that the lesser clergy recognised on which side their bread was buttered and acted accordingly.

In parliamentary debates, it was important for the government to be sure at least of a certain number of votes, and where better than from the compliant bishops who were only there because their political views were sure and unchanging.

By the end of the eighteenth century, with so corrupt and corrupting a system of preferment, the number of outstanding men in the Church inevitably grew less, and there was a general complacency that it should be so. 'Enthusiasm' was suspect, for 'peace and propriety were the qualities which the eighteenth-century Church desired, and such as threatened to disturb the one or outrage the other were deeply suspect'.[3]

The nineteenth century was no better, though the generally Tory clergy became uneasy at the appointments made by Whig prime ministers, and Whig prime ministers found it difficult to find enough Whig clergymen of suitable calibre. But it was Lord Melbourne's attempt to appoint an Oxford Whig, Dr Hampden, as regius professor of divinity (he had thought of making him a bishop but a suitable see was not available) which produced so adverse a reaction that for the first time serious criticism arose against the method of appointing bishops. Though the resistance at Oxford to the appointment was ostensibly against Hampden (for an unorthodoxy of doctrine which into today's theological climate would have caused hardly a ripple), it was indirectly an attack on the royal supremacy and on Melbourne, to frighten him against making a like appointment to the bench of bishops.

Duly frightened, Melbourne in future sought to appoint Whig clergymen who yet would command the respect of the Tory clergy, which proved not an easy task. In the spring of 1836, three bishops died, and 'the mortality of bishops at such a crisis' was welcomed by Whigs. Melbourne's enquiries were once described in this fashion:

'Is he a good man?'
'An excellent man: he is a most accomplished theologian, and exemplary clergyman, and is truly beloved throughout his district . . . '
'But is he a good man – is he a good Whig – will he vote for the Irish Corporation Bill?'[4]

It is not unlike the fictional conversation between the Appointments Secretary and the Prime Minister in the BBC's *Yes Minister*:

'He has an eminently suitable wife, Prime Minister.'
'You mean she's devout, does good works?'
'No, no! I mean she's the daughter of the Earl of Chichester.'

As a Tory, Robert Peel had more choice than he needed, and commanded sufficient votes already in the House of Lords to allow him to exercise the principle he recognised that to raise Church patronage above party politics would in the end be to the benefit of his party. Even so, he would not elevate Puseyites, and good bishops were lost to the Church.

Palmerston was even more determined to move in the opposite direction to that of the Puseyite Oxford Movement and its suspicious high-churchery. But he did believe that a bishop should not make party speeches in the House of Lords, that he should not be learned but rather should be a simple, godly pastor of the people. It was no bad aspiration, and he found many in the evangelical party who fitted the job description; but it was not popular in the Church of England, and the bishops it produced were often mocked.

Chadwick comments that

This monochrome of patronage was no friend to evangelicals in the Church of England. It lifted them from the pulpit or school where they offered words of life and buttoned them in a pillory of gaiters.[5]

Other voices, such as that of the Earl of Aberdeen, were beginning to suggest that because there were theological groupings within the Church, so these groupings should be represented among the bishops, so long as they were sincere, honest and moderate (and not high-churchmen of the Puseyite variety). It probably did no harm to the growing influence of the Oxford Movement, as the devotion and self-sacrifice of clergy of that ilk, serving in the hardest parishes among the poor and dispossessed, suffering persecution and imprisonment for their views, probably advanced their cause more satisfactorily than if their leaders had become bishops.

And in later years, there were more catholics among the bishops than evangelicals, and in the 1950s and 1960s it was the latter who themselves had much cause for complaint. But the bishops, up to the decade before the setting up of the Crown Appointments Commission, did have giants among their number – Kirk of Oxford, Mortimer of Essex, Michael Ramsey of Durham, York and Canterbury, Ian Ramsey of Durham, Williams of Leicester to name a few.

But these were still the appointments of a secular state, made by a Prime Minister who might now not even be a Christian, let alone a member of the Church of England, and it is hardly surprising that voices were increasingly raised against the impropriety of such a system.

It was not until 1978 that the appointment of bishops came more clearly into the hands of the Church. The agreement between the Church and Prime Minister Callaghan (and it was and is no more than an agreement) that there be a Crown Appointments Commission consisting of the two archbishops, six elected members of the General Synod and four elected from the Vacancy of See committee of the diocese concerned, meant that at least the two names submitted to the Prime Minister were the choice of the Church.

There were initially fears that this would undermine the established status of the Church, though it is arguable that it need be no part of disestablishment if neither the Prime Minister nor the Crown had any part in the appointment of the Church's chief pastors. Against this it is argued that because a diocesan bishop will one day, if he survives long enough, have a seat in the House of Lords, the Crown must have some part in his appointment. It would certainly be a sad reflection on the nation's attitude to things spiritual if the Lords Spiritual were to be excluded from Parliament.

Unfortunately, the system has tended to produce bishops who are the least likely to have strong views on any subject, and that in itself not surprisingly raises doubts from Anglicans and non-Anglicans alike about their right to seats in the House of Lords. In the present state of the Church of England – not to mention the multi-faith character of the nation – it is right that questions are raised about the propriety of confining the Lords Spiritual to bishops of the Church of England.

But there are deeper questions here, about the nature of the bishop's primary role as chief pastor to a diocese, about the quasi-political role which some expect of a bishop, and this leadership aspect deserves a chapter to itself. For the remainder of this chapter we must consider, not the style of leadership required of a Church leader, but the efficacy of the present system which endows them with that function.

I was ordained in 1955, and in those days it was unlikely that anyone would be considered for high office without a public school/Oxbridge background. Even among ordinands, the class barriers were retained implicitly at any rate: I was advised (and it was right advice), as a lower-middle-class lad with a Lancashire accent, to avoid seeking entry to Cuddesdon or Westcott House theological colleges. As a pattern for the Church of God it was indefensible. But it did produce a bench of bishops of a calibre unquestionably higher than anything we have had in more recent years.

And the better men among them did not want or seek to be bishops. When Michael Ramsey, then regius professor at Cambridge, was offered the see of Durham by Winston Churchill, he was minded to refuse, though in his deep spirituality he knew he must consider if this was the will of God for him. Owen Chadwick records[6] that having read the biography of Archbishop Randall Davidson, Ramsey had found it very depressing: 'the wire-pulling, the hedging, and energy spent on things that don't matter, and all the sitting on the fence'.[6] But his reading of the life of Bishop Charles Gore showed him that it could also be inspiring.

Archbishop Fisher did not much want Ramsey to go to Durham, and when Ramsey asked him how important he considered it to be that scholarly men became bishops, Fisher replied that he did not think it mattered to any great extent. But Ramsey had come to the opposite view, and felt that the bench was not well served in this area: 'If you walked from Humber to Severn and dodged Derby,' he had commented to a friend, 'you would not find a bishop who could read or write.'[7] In consequence, Fisher's dismissal of the importance of scholarship on the bench strengthened Ramsey's growing feeling that he must accept the offer of the bishopric of Durham.

He was nonetheless irritated with the direction in which vocation was driving him.

On 17 June 1952, a Fellow of Magdalene College walked down Trinity Street in Cambridge and was suddenly aware of the regius professor of divinity waddling ahead of him and throwing his arms about and muttering gloomily to himself, 'Hell! Hell!' 'Why, what's the matter?' 'The Lord works in mysterious ways! I am to be Bishop of Durham.'[8]

Perhaps it was the fact of a vocation accepted but not sought which helped to make him the greatest archbishop of this century; just as Bishop George Bell's courage during the Second World War in speaking out against the destruction of German cities, ensuring Churchill's absolute opposition to his elevation to Canterbury, made Bell the greatest archbishop who never was. The contrast between Bell and Ramsey on the one hand and the majority of the present bench of bishops on the other could not be more marked.

In Ramsey's day, the convention which had developed between the wars was that the Archbishop of Canterbury would submit three names to the Prime Minister, who need not recommend the first (or any of the three) to the Crown. So far as Ramsey was concerned, the prime minister of the day almost always did as the archbishop desired, though two factors made Ramsey feel less free than he would have liked to have been.

The Prime Minister had a constitutional right to interfere in appointments, even though such interference by the secular into the spiritual was seen to be offensive by many in the Church. But there was also the Patronage Secretary, who had no constitutional right to interfere but had developed great power to do so by virtue of his position. Michael Ramsey recognised the ability and thoroughness of those who held the position of the Prime Minister's Appointments Secretary, but saw the dangers in the system.

In an essay on 'Church and State', he wrote:

It is likely that with such a system there will be many sound nominations, likely also that there may from time to time be an inspired nomination like that of Ian Ramsey to Durham. It is also certain that there will be strange 'non-appointments' and chances missed – for the knowledge is filtered through the mind of one man, and no man is without his prejudices and blind spots.[9]

Now that the Church, through the Crown Appointments Commission, sends two names to the Prime Minister, the choice is more certainly that of the Church. Even so, it is the Appointments Secretary who speaks for the names when they are presented to the Prime Minister, and there is a barrier of confidentiality placed over what happens once the names leave the Commission, a barrier which could be unhealthy. Certainly because 'no man is without his prejudices and blind spots', it is arguable that, just as no one may serve on the Commission for more than ten years, no appointments secretary should serve more than five.

Yet even though the establishment of the Crown Appointments Commission gave the wider Church a real voice in episcopal appointments and worked well under Archbishop Coggan, the criticism against the bishops appointed in the decade of the Eighties during the primacy of Robert Runcie was far greater than before the Commission existed.

It was bound to become more public than the growing private gossip of senior clergy and it eventually burst forth in an unexpected manner. A long tradition had been established that *Crockford's Clerical Directory* began with an anonymous preface which surveyed the state of the Church of England through one person's eyes. As such it was sometimes trenchant and personal in its comments, and an important means by which the leadership of the Church learnt what people were really saying, rather than being told only what they wanted to hear, which is too often their normal diet.

But with the growing ascendancy of liberalism within the Church, it was usually conservative leaders who were criticised by liberals rather than the other way around. Thus in the 1977/79 Preface, Archbishop Donald Coggan was described by the Preface's arch-liberal author, David Edwards, as a man who rides out 'with his mind made up, as a latter-day Don Quixote, and there has not been the sense that there was in his predecessor's time of the Primate as the more edifying type of Canterbury pilgrim'.

Earlier, in 1973, the author had attacked Archbishop Fisher, still warm in his grave, for a misuse of retirement.

Few figures prominent in public life can have made themselves such an embarrassment to their successors . . . He compared other bishops as housemasters, though some of them felt at times that they were treated as fourth-form boys.

But in the 1987 Preface, the author who in the end was revealed as Canon Gareth Bennett, a historian from New College, Oxford, committed the unforgivable sin: as a conservative, he attacked the liberal establishment, and in particular Dr Robert Runcie, Archbishop of Canterbury. The furore it produced eventually drove Canon Bennett to suicide. Having quoted an MP's comment that Dr Runcie is 'usually found to be nailing his colours to the fence', he went on to suggest that the archbishop was therefore 'peculiarly vulnerable to pressure groups'.

His criticisms of appointments during the Runcie primacy were the most pungent:

> His clear preference is for men of liberal disposition with a moderately Catholic style which is not taken to the point of having firm principles. If in addition they have a good appearance and are articulate over the media he is prepared to overlook a certain theological deficiency. Dr Runcie and his closest associates are men who have nothing to prevent them following what they think is the wish of the majority of the moment.

To those of us who had served with Dr Runcie during his ten years as Bishop of St Albans, there seemed nothing exceptional in this judgment, and our personal affection for the man as well as our admiration of his other qualities as bishop were not dimmed because we recognised that Bennett had highlighted some of his weaknesses. No one is without an Achilles heel, and one of the penalties of high office is that characteristics which would be hidden in a lesser role are likely to be revealed for the world to see.

As for the criticisms of appointments, I was interviewed on BBC Radio 4's *Today* programme on the morning of the Preface's publication and was asked if I was surprised as what had appeared. I commented that the surprise was not that it had been said, but that it had not been said until now. The most cursory glance at many of the appointments made up until that time in the Runcie primacy showed clearly that they were indeed 'men of liberal disposition with a moderately catholic style which [was] not taken to the point of having firm principles'.

But was it nepotism? I thought so at first, for certainly most, not only of the diocesan bishops, but also for the deans, provosts and suffragan bishops, were men who had had close contact during their careers with Dr Runcie; indeed, many had been brought by him into the diocese of St Albans during his time there as bishop. They were uniformly liberal in their views but not by any means all of an equal calibre. Yet by the time the Preface was published I had discounted nepotism as too facile an answer to the problem.

In a speech in the General Synod I said:

> The situation is undoubtedly scandalous, and it has gravely damaged the comprehensive character of the Church of England: maybe only the Prime Minister can put it right; but the cause is much more serious and fundamental than that suggested in the Preface and that is at the very heart of our problem.[10]

It was, I suggested, partly through a mistaken belief that the differences within the Church of England were like a straight line, with anglo-catholics at the one end and evangelicals at the other, with the liberals comfortably in the middle. If those consulted about a senior appointment said, 'We don't want an extremist, we want someone who is middle of the road,' who then is left but the liberal?

But the Church of England is not like a straight line but rather is a triangle. There are three extremes, catholic, evangelical and liberal, and most of its members are somewhere in the middle, inclining to one or another but at a greater or lesser distance from the points of the triangle. The almost exclusive concentration on a narrow group of elitist liberals in the appointments made in the first seven years of the Runcie primacy totally changed the character of the Church of England, and is the major cause of the present crisis in which it finds itself. More important to this study is the effect which it had on the style of leadership which developed as a result.

Of the eighteenth-century clergy, Moorman had written: 'Clergy who were ambitious, as indeed most of them were, knew how to play their cards and obtain preferment.'[11] To be born a member of a noble family or to become tutor or chaplain in such a household was no longer a qualification, but certainly the ambitious cleric would still need 'to preach the right kind of sermons, publish the right kind of pamphlets'. 'Peace and propriety were the qualities which the eighteenth-century Church desired, and such as threatened to disturb the one or outrage the other were deeply suspect,'[12] and again little had changed if for 'peace and propriety' were substituted the words 'to promote views consonant with the tenor of the secular world and not rock the liberal boat'.

When BBC Television's *Yes, Prime Minister* featured the issue of the appointment of bishops, there was a delightful moment when the qualifications of one possible candidate were presented to the Prime Minister. He had been a diocesan adviser in ethnic communities and Secretary for Social Responsibility, had organised conferences on inter-faith interface, between Christians and Marxists and between Christians and the women of Greenham Common. He was now Secretary of the Disarmament Committee of the British Council of Churches.

'But has he ever been an ordinary vicar of a parish?' asked the Prime Minister.

'Good heavens, Prime Minister,' was the reply, 'clergymen who want to be bishops try and avoid pastoral work.'

It was a portrayal near enough to the mark to be distinctly uncomfortable viewing for members of the bench of bishops and hysterically funny for everyone else.

As Edmund Burke declared, 'Well is it known that ambition can creep as well as soar,'[13] and the more serious aspect is the corrupting effect which the need to compromise has had on ambitious clergy in their often desperate quest for preferment. Principles have been sacrificed at the drop of a hat, and since some bishops have applied the same criteria to their internal diocesan appointments as those in vogue for senior posts, speeches

have been made in local as well as national synods, articles
written, brownie points gained, all to climb a ladder which
ought not to exist at all in the Church of God. In the end,
the victim is integrity, and a clergyman without integrity
is a sorry creature.

There is no sign of improvement. Recently a young
priest was visited by his suffragan bishop, to talk about
his work in the parish and about his future. In five years,
his average Sunday congregation had increased by 60 per
cent, and in addition on certain Sundays an outreach
service to those on the fringe of church life brought in
as many again. On Easter Day there were almost five
hundred people in church, which was about 7 per cent
of the population of his suburban parish. In these days
of declining numbers, few churches could approach this,
and in fact it was the seventh highest Easter number in his
diocese.

'But you'll never get another job in this diocese,' the
suffragan bishop told him. The young priest was not
looking for a move but wondered what he had done
wrong. 'You are disloyal to the diocesan bishop,' he
was told. He was a priest whose faith was based firmly
in the teachings of scripture and he held to the creeds
without question, totally loyal to the fundamental beliefs
of the Church of England, and his disloyalty was that
he had publicly criticised the bishop for only appointing
those whose faith and teaching openly questioned those
fundamentals. 'If I have to choose between being loyal
to my bishop and loyal to my Lord, it is not a choice,'
was his response. There is evidence that such an attitude
is widespread and it bodes ill for the future leadership of
the Church of England.

Moreover it represents an attitude which is gravely
damaging the Church today, whatever it does for the
future. A senior priest was asked to consider a post in
America, and though he was interested, he wanted if
possible to give his service and whatever gifts he had to

the Church of England which had nurtured his faith and his vocation. He endeavoured to discover if he was likely to be given any senior appointment in England and such was the curious response that he sought out a friendly bishop to make his own enquiries. The answer came eventually: 'You will never get any kind of preferment in the Church of England because you have the reputation that you can't get on with people.' In reality he had been appointed to his present post precisely to heal damaged relationships and had successfully preserved the particular community which he served from being closed. But there it was on his record and nothing would remove it.

In any institution or profession, there is no one without enemies. Thus if it is desired that a promotion be blocked, it is always possible to find the right person to make a sufficiently damaging statement which will effectively block any further progress. At least in the armed forces, where a commanding officer will make an annual assessment of his staff, the person assessed has the right to see what is said about him and if necessary to challenge it. In the Church, the cult of confidentiality prevents this, and the jealous bitchiness of many of the clergy about their colleagues means that injustice is perpetuated.

Naked ambition, inadequacies in the assessment system, the knowledge that compliance gains more than principle, secrecy in the mechanism – all inhibit the development of strong leadership in the Church of England. But two other factors do more damage than all the rest combined: the concept of collegiality and the dynamics by which the Crown Appointments Commission operates.

It was particularly during the Runcie primacy that the concept of episcopal collegiality developed. Rather like the Prime Minister's Cabinet, where no one steps out of line (save when the antennae of ambition notice the approach of a leadership election) in order to safeguard corporate policy and responsibility, so the bishops have come to adopt a similar process.

In the Church, the cause may be weak leadership, in
that a strong leader can cope with difference, knowing
that it is more creative than destructive. Or it may be to
give a false picture of unity preserved in times of division
and difficulty, in the mistaken belief that disharmony
is somehow unchristian. Its effect is to curb the more
traditional and theologically conservative bishops, while
allowing free rein to the wilder liberals to propound views
which are often on the very fringes of orthodoxy. And
in the appointment of bishops, it would be a somewhat
dubious quality of character to seek in candidates for
higher office. Ready compliance can be the enemy of
true leadership.

In 1992, I was elected by the House of Clergy to the
General Synod to serve for five years on the Crown
Appointments System, so I am constrained by the very
secrecy I have criticised. Not that confidentiality is not a
vital part of the process: it would not be good for a man
to know that he had been considered for a bishopric and
turned down – not once but maybe more than once. And
for one appointment there might be a number of suitable
candidates, while for another, needing other qualities,
those same men might be quite unsuitable.

Members need to be able to comment with absolute
frankness on the names which come before them, entirely
without fear that anything which is said will be repeated
outside the confines of the Commission. That in itself can
be a small safeguard against dismissing a candidate on the
grounds of a malicious comment made in the process
leading up to the meeting. By a curious mental quirk
brought on by the confidentiality, I find that a few days
after the Commission has met I have anyway completely
forgotten at least one of the two names sent forward to
the Prime Minister.

What can be said is that the meeting of the Commission
has three phases. After a solemn undertaking has been
given not to reveal which names have been considered,

nor who has said what about them, consideration is given to the statement of needs produced from within the vacant diocese. Then we look at the memorandum put together by the appointments secretaries from their own consultations. After this, the candidates whose names have been sent in (every member has this right) are examined both in relation to their potential as bishop of the vacant diocese and to the contribution which they might make to the wider Church.

By the end of the first evening, it will be expected that a short list of five or six names will be left, which are again considered at the morning session, together with any discarded names which members may wish to bring back. Further names may then be eliminated, after which there is a complicated process of voting. With the exception of the two appointments secretaries who are non-voting members, all the members, both from the diocese and the Synod together with the two archbishops, take part in this with equal voting rights.

Voting is secret, and at the end two names remain, cach with a two-thirds vote in favour of that name. The Commission can express its preferences to the Prime Minister by placing the names in an ordcr of priority, if it so chooses.

People have commented to me that the new Commission has begun to produce bishops subtly different from those who came to office as a result of the previous Commissions, and I am too closely involved to recognise whether or not this is so. There are those who in any case would argue that since the Holy Spirit is the source of the Commission's guidance, whichever bishops are chosen are the choice neither of the Commission nor of the Prime Minister and Her Majesty but of God himself.

We must however be cautious in referring to God's Holy Spirit, for he is often the justification which Christians claim for decisions they wished to make for human rather than divine reasons. In anothcr part of the Anglican

Communion, where the diocesan bishop is appointed by an electoral college, I was told by a member of such a college of the process of prayer, silence, discussion, then more of the same repeated over a period of twenty-four hours, with all of it requiring that the weeks of lobbying beforehand for particular candidates be put completely out of mind. In the end, one candidate emerged as the clear choice and the members of the college remarked on how wonderful it had been to 'feel' the Holy Spirit at work among them. Unfortunately before he could be consecrated, the candidate suffered a heart attack and died.

Perhaps a real trust in the guidance of God's Holy Spirit in the appointment of a bishop would be to follow the example of the Apostles in seeking a replacement of the traitor Judas: 'And they cast lots for them, and the lot fell on Matthias; and he was enrolled with the eleven apostles.'[14]

Or maybe to re-enact the appointment of St Fabian as Bishop of Rome, of whom it is said that when the brethren were assembled for the election, a dove flew into the church and was seen to settle upon the head of Fabian. The congregation cried out, 'Fabian for bishop!' and he was immediately consecrated and enthroned, serving for sixteen years until his martyrdom in AD 250. Birdseed on the head of a candidate would then be as reprehensible as dirt in the pocket of a Test cricketer.

I do believe that the Holy Spirit is at work in the Crown Appointments Commission, but I would hesitate at the presumption of suggesting that our every choice is not really our own but his. Every member is hindered by the reality of human sinfulness, which obscures the purity of God's guidance. The Holy Spirit's main role in the process, as in much of the Church's activity, is either to make the best of what has been decided or, at worst, to clear up the mess we have left behind, just as he makes up for the deficiencies which each of us bears within us in any work to which he has called us.

But in assessing the results of the Commission's work, this means that it would be a foolish mistake to sit back complacently on the assumption that the choices made are the responsibility not of the Commission but of God himself. Human inadequacy, human prejudice, and the sheer impossibility of total human impartiality will inevitably intrude into the process. If there is a weakness there, then human nature will exploit it, and the weakness of this system is that it must tend to produce 'safe' men. In that there is nothing new; the author of the *Crockford's* Preface of 1955/56 commented on the earlier system:

> We wonder also whether the selection of bishops is not governed by too great a desire for safety and whether risks in regard to opinions, youth, and old age might not more often be taken.

As a member of the Commission, it would be improper for me to comment on the process involved in selecting the names which are presented to the Prime Minister. But its dynamics can be as clear to a non-member as to an 'insider', and there is nothing in the proper requirement for confidentiality which inhibits me therefore from examining this aspect.

And it is the dynamics of the system which must militate against unusual appointments or the kind of 'inspired' appointment which Archbishop Michael Ramsey recognised in Ian Ramsey's elevation to Durham, as surely as in the old system which it replaced. Its design means it will tend to produce the same 'safe' men, now able to fit into the collegiality of the House of Bishops without discomfort to themselves or to others.

The election of three members from the House of Clergy and three from the Laity was intended to give the three wings, catholic, evangelical and liberal, a representative voice on the Commission, and in this it has so far succeeded, though with the marginalisation of orthodox catholics as a result of the ordination of women, it is unlikely that this will continue after the next election to the Commission.

In addition to these six who with the two archbishops make up the central membership, four are elected by the vacant diocese whose bishop is to be appointed. This they do well, and the local knowledge of needs and opportunities is important in finding the right man for the job. But it would be unnatural if a diocese, while it might recognise the need for unusual and experimental appointments for the good of the Church as a whole, did not say, in effect, 'but not in our backyard'.

If the charge in the 1955/56 Preface was just – and it was undoubtedly just – it is sad that, even with a system which gives the Church itself more say, little has changed in forty years. The questions raised by the writer of that Preface are, with only slight adjustment, as pertinent in 1995 as they were in 1955:

> Does not the accident of having been brought up in the entourage of some prominent person, or in some particular family [we might now say, 'theological college'] or social circle, still unduly increase one's chances of becoming a bishop? Are there not able persons who, because of their own modesty or because their views are out of favour in the diocese in which they serve, remain in undeserved obscurity, the full use of their talents being lost to the Church at a time when men of distinction are so greatly needed?

At least the old system produced men like Ian Ramsey, Robert Mortimer, Graham Leonard, Kenneth Kirk, and Michael Ramsey. Since men of their ilk seem not to exist today, it is perhaps hypothetical to wonder if under the present system even they would have been passed over. And the real mavericks like Hugh Montefiore and Mervyn Stockwood would almost certainly have been *personae non grata*.

It does appear that we are in a Catch 22 situation. The Church desperately needs a more dynamic leadership which no system of appointments is likely to produce; and if it could, where are the candidates?

10

Leadership in the Church

Think'st thou that duty shall have dread to speak
When power to flattery bows?
King Lear, I.i.149

In early 1988, I received a letter quite out of the blue from the Archbishop of York, Dr Habgood, inviting me to become Archdeacon of York. I had felt some four years before then that I ought to move on from Bushey Heath on the northern edge of London, the parish where I had served for some fourteen years, but for a long time nothing came my way. Or rather a number of interesting and senior posts appeared on the horizon and then floated out of my ken as swiftly as they had floated in.

I had known that the combination of my background and my beliefs would bar me from episcopal office and since I enjoyed being a parish priest – as well as being of the firm conviction that career and promotion should have no place in the priestly vocation – I was little concerned. The Bishop of St Albans thought otherwise, and told me that I would never be a bishop because I 'didn't get on with people' (curiously these were precisely the same words used of the priest in similar circumstances described in Chapter 9).

But I had sought election to the Crown Appointments Commission twice, whose membership effectively bars one from the bench of bishops, and years before when Dr Runcie had told me my name was on 'the list', I had talked to Archbishop Michael Ramsey during a priests' retreat, asking if I really would have to accept a suffragan bishopric if I were offered it.

I mention this now because it is a popular method of dealing with clerical critics of the episcopal establishment to say that they are disappointed men, disappointed that is at not gaining the same preferment themselves.

By the time Dr Habgood's letter came, I had accepted a small parish near St Albans, the village of Flamstead. It had a beautiful medieval church and, more important, a long tradition of the kind of teaching that I believe to be fundamental to the mission and witness of the Church. As a family, we looked forward to spending the remainder of my ministry before retirement with the kind and welcoming people of Flamstead, even though a *Daily Mail* editorial had described it as the equivalent of a dissident priest being sent to Siberia, and in spite of the diocesan authorities making it clear that if I did not accept, there would be nothing else.

Because I had felt this was what God wanted me to do, I took three months to decide that maybe I ought to accept the archbishop's offer. But from the day I received his letter, I did know that if he could offer me such a post, he was the sort of man I should like to work with, because he clearly represented the sort of Church of England I had known and loved, but which now seemed to be disappearing.

For John Habgood and I had had our very public differences, not least on the suicide of Canon Gareth Bennett and the events which led up to it, and I had said on television that the adverse comments which he had made on the then-anonymous author of the *Crockford's* Preface and the manner in which they were presented showed that Habgood was quite unsuitable to become Archbishop of Canterbury. Yet he was not only prepared to offer me a senior post in his diocese but ready to cope with the higher national profile it would give a priest not known for reticence in public comment.

The encouragement of dissent is not a characteristic common to the present bench of bishops of the Church of England. The most divisive issue to come before the Church in recent years has been the matter of the ordination of women to the priesthood, and this is not the place for a consideration of that, either in its process, its theology or its consequence. But it must be noted that its divisiveness encouraged bishops who supported the proposals not to appoint to their senior staffs (that is as suffragan bishop or archdeacon) and, in the more extreme cases, nor to large parishes as rector or vicar, otherwise able men who were of an opposing viewpoint to the diocesan bishop.

Anglican clergy of the present day have among their number those ready to compromise for the sake of pre-ferment, and in that nothing has changed in the Church's history. In itself it makes for weak leadership in the Church, in the same way that a policeman who accepts a bribe undermines the integrity of the whole body. The ability of a leader to cope with disagreement is in reality a sign of strength, not of weakness, for dissent at its best is creative.

Any relationship grows when disagreement is faced and overcome. Husband and wife will inevitably reach points in their relationship, because it is so close, where differences on minor and major issues will threaten its stability and sometimes its continuance. But in working through such differences – even if sometimes they can only agree to disagree – they deepen both the relationship they have and the love they share. It is the refusal to accept the reality and content of the dissent, and the deliberate silence that marks a denial of its importance, which is the real threat to the relationship and to the love that is its foundation.

Yet within Church circles, conflict is so often seen as something to be avoided at all costs. In that late and quite unlamented body, the British Council of Churches, on whose assembly I served for nine long and frustrating years, superficial agreement was ever preferred to real ding-dong discussion. To put in a critical amendment was to undermine the authority of the executive, and endless efforts would be made to find a form of words which could be accepted by both sides in an argument, even though the interpretation might be contrary to each.

The General Synod of the Church of England can fall into the same trap. In November 1987, the Synod debated a Private Member's motion, introduced by the Revd Tony Higton, on homosexuality. The motion reaffirmed the biblical standard 'given for the well-being of society', that 'fornication, adultery and homosexual acts are sinful in all circumstances', going on to demand that Christian leaders be 'exemplary' in all spheres of morality, and ending with a call to the Church 'to show Christ-like compassion to those who have fallen into sexual sin'.[1]

On the face of it, it was a simple restatement of scriptural standards, both of morality and of compassion. But the Synod – or at least the strong liberal element within it – is ever suspicious of Tony Higton, an uncompromising evangelical who is unfashionable enough to believe that the Bible is true and relevant to the 1990s.

The debate followed a pattern familiar to Synod watchers. After Higton's introduction, a layman was called, a doctor with expertise in genito-urinary disease who supported the motion. He was followed by another supporting speech from the then Bishop of London, Dr Graham Leonard, and after that came a vigorous attack from a spokesman for the gay community. Then the temporising began, first with a might-be-this/might-be-that speech, from Dr Runcie, yet to retire from Canterbury, after which the debate was sprinkled with characteristic contributions which damned with faint praise.

The ground was thus carefully prepared for the Bishop of Chester's amendment. Bishop Baughan is a gentle, kindly evangelical, a man of integrity and so clearly without guile that he would imagine fellow-Christians to be as honest as he is himself. His amendment appeared to be a clear restatement of Christian sexual morality, affirming traditional teaching.[2] In particular it affirmed that sexual intercourse as an act of total commitment belonged '*properly* within a permanent married relationship', that fornication and adultery were '*sins against* this ideal, to be met by a call to repentance and the exercise of compassion', that 'homosexual acts *also fall short of* this ideal, and are likewise to be met by a call to repentance and the exercise of compassion', and that all Christians, especially those in leadership, should be exemplary in their behaviour (emphasis added).

It was passed by a huge majority of 408 to 8, with 13 abstentions. But in reality the Synod (and the bishop) had been outmanoeuvred and outgunned. In his speech, the bishop was quite clear that his understanding of the amendment was as an expression of the traditional Christian, biblical stance on sexual morality.[3]

Heterosexual promiscuity or the promotion of homosexual genital acts and even so-called 'homosexual marriages' are not only a sordid falling short but are contrary to and incompatible with the grace and holiness of God:

By way of further elucidation, he went on:

By emphasising holiness in my amendment, we also affirm the very many genuine homosexually orientated people who do live for the Lord without genital acts, often with great courage, and who give so much love and care and support to the Church's life.[4]

But it was not that interpretation, totally unacceptable to many liberals in the Synod, which gained it so great a majority. Rather it was the inclusion of certain words and phrases which by their ambiguity, clearly unintended by the Bishop of Chester, enabled the pro-gay lobby to put their own interpretation on the final motion. If sexual intercourse as an act of total commitment could be said to belong '*properly* within a permanent married relationship' (emphasis added), the implication could be that though this was the norm, sexual intercourse might also be acceptable behaviour outside a permanent married relationship.

In the same way, though the motion as amended states that 'fornication and adultery are *sins against* this ideal' and that 'homosexual acts *also fall short of* this ideal' (emphasis added), the motion is careful not to categorise homosexual acts as 'sin'. Unlike fornication and adultery which are 'sins against' the ideal which God has set, homosexual acts simply 'fall short' of this ideal. It might be argued that this alternation of words was merely for the avoidance of tautology, since that which falls short of God's ideal is sin.

That is certainly the interpretation which many who voted for the motion would have placed upon it. But in reality it was a clever and successful attempt to provide a motion on a delicate issue so worded that the appearance of division could be avoided. The Synod could have given a clear indication of its attitude, one way or another, on a moral issue – or even that there was deep disagreement – but instead preferred to duck the issue entirely. That is not Christian leadership, but is more akin to the behaviour of a political party desperate to avoid the appearance of division in the run-up to an election. At least for the politician there is the perfectly reasonable excuse of pragmatism.

The fear of disagreement is exacerbated by the concept of collegiality, which has been adopted so enthusiastically by the House of Bishops. To add to the problem, there is now always an 'official' line on controversial issues, which bishops are encouraged to follow. This was revealed in the annual report for 1993 of the General Synod Committee for Communications, a highly competent body with a small but very able and energetic staff in Church House, Westminster, presently chaired by the Bishop of Wakefield, the Rt Revd Nigel McCulloch.

The report describes how, during 1993, a diocesan communications officer received a complaint from a journalist from one of the Sunday tabloid newspapers. Her task had been to telephone bishops for their opinions on a particular issue, and her complaint was that they were all giving the same answer. The author of the report, Bishop McCulloch, comments:

> This story illustrates the greater cohesion that has developed when we respond as a church to particular stories. The Communications Unit agrees a line with the relevant board, council or archbishop and this is circulated to bishops and DCOs [diocesan communications officers].[5]

This astonishing admission is slightly tempered by the words which follow:

> Of course, individual bishops will decide whether to use the line or not when speaking to the media. There will be occasions when a diversity of views will be expressed; and rightly so.

But with the firm principle of collegiality, the peer pressure from fellow-bishops will inevitably restrict the possibility that a 'diversity of views' is likely to be expressed.

In other words, bishops are not only encouraged by the principle of collegiality to avoid rocking the boat, but are in some instances actually given the lines to speak, like an actor playing a part. It would be interesting to know just how far this is taken, and it does explain the unanimity of episcopal response when I raised the question of the behaviour of the Prince of Wales.

No less than six bishops emphasised in similar words that I had commented on a hypothetical situation. And more than one bishop stressed the importance of remembering that George Austin was 'only' the archdeacon of York and consequently not really to be taken at all as seriously as someone as important as a bishop.

One one diocesan bishop stood against the advice from on high on that occasion. The Bishop of Sodor and Man, the Rt Revd Noel Jones (a former chaplain of the fleet and well used to dealing with both admirals and royals) commented – quite against the trend – that 'it would be right for us to say that anyone who aspires to a position of real high office must also have really high morals. If I had a future monarch who was divorced I would find it very difficult to say I was giving allegiance to that person.'

But a former Archbishop of Canterbury, Dr Donald Coggan, in retirement and therefore not on the Church House mailing list, was more forthright in his expression of Christian principle than serving bishops: 'If a person has broken the marriage vows they took in the presence of God, then repentance is called for, and that applies as much to the Royal household as it does to the chap who sweeps the streets.'

The suffragan Bishops of Kensington and Crediton added their support, the late John Hughes of Kensington going much further than I had done. 'The Church,' he said, 'might well remind him that the Royal Family is fighting for its credibility. Some attempt to repair his family life would be the best example he could give to the nation. If he married a divorcee, he would have to renounce the Crown.'

But it was archdeacons, unencumbered by collegiality or party lines ladled out from on high, who came out most strongly in my support. The Archdeacon of Canterbury, Michael Till, warned that the Prince of Wales's credibility was under threat. 'There is a question mark and whether that fades into silence or is consolidated depends upon the next weeks, months, years.' As for divorce and remarriage, Till added: 'I think the Church would find it difficult to handle, as would the congregations.'

David Robinson, Archdeacon of Blackburn, said he would be unhappy to 'have a king as head of the Church of England who took a very liberal view of marriage'. Timothy Stevens, Archdeacon of West Ham, supported him: 'There would be many in the Church of England who would argue that to marry a divorcee would make it untenable for him to be head of the church.'

The Archdeacon of Chesterfield, Gerald Phizakerley, was equally firm:

> There will be those who will be very disappointed that the full ideals and standards of Christian family life are not being embodied. I think those people would not want him to be head of the church . . . an icon of family life is tarnished.

Polls began to be taken by newspapers, and these consistently showed that public opinion was massively with the archdeacons rather than the bishops, at least of the order of two to one. Unfortunately, the episcopal party-line did not confine itself to dismissing the issue (and possibly the Archdeacon of York with it) as hypothetical.

One bishop described the Prince's alleged adultery as a 'mere peccadillo', while the Bishop of Truro, Michael Ball, complained that 'the British people have a hang-up about certain aspects of morality. All right, that aspect may be tied up with vows but, in many ways, I consider that a moral cul-de-sac.' He went on to point out that morality is a community as well as a personal affair: 'Housing and social issues are just as much about right and wrong.' So they are, but it is curious that a bishop is ready to ignore sins in one department of life and not in another.

One forthright bishop suggested that I had asked for the Prince's head on a charger, that Charles's behaviour was no one else's business, that he had been a fool about his marriage. He should have stuck with Camilla or finished with her sooner, but 'all chaps have a rush to the head'. His advice to Charles was to 'keep his head down, don't talk about politics, do a bit of shooting, and in a couple of years it will all be forgotten'. It was more like a sympathetic colonel remembering his own wild youth when dealing with a young subaltern caught in the bushes with the landlord's daughter, than a bishop of the Church of God interpreting the demands of the gospel of God entrusted to his care.

Others on the episcopal bench took a different line. The Archbishop of York implied that it was just another example of my lusting after media exposure ('well-known for his readiness to speak to the media'), while the Bishop of Norwich, Peter Nott, sniggered that the Archdeacon of York had 'lots of eccentric views'.[6]

In fact, on this occasion I came off rather lightly in that respect. In 1991, after I had preached a controversial sermon in York Minster, the Archbishop of York compared me to the Fat Boy of *Pickwick Papers* who crept up on an old lady saying 'I wants to make your flesh creep.' I had suggested that waiting in the wings of the women priests' debate were further controversial issues, such as the recognition of homosexuality as an acceptable Christian lifestyle, the use of feminist language for God in our liturgies, and similar matters, in all of which, some three years later, I am beginning to be proved accurate in my predictions. The contempt which poured forth from episcopal mouths and pens on that occasion would be yet more disturbing if it were the result of what the Committee for Communications describes as 'the greater cohesion which has developed when we respond as a church to particular stories', with an official line issued from above.

Now that the Committee has revealed its procedures, it would be an even greater cause for concern if this were the reason for the almost unanimous style of response to Canon Gareth Bennett's comments in the *Crockford's* Preface of 1987. Interestingly, the first to be made did come from the then Chairman of the Communications Committee, the Bishop of St Albans, John Taylor, who read from a prepared statement to a senior Press Association journalist, Reg Evans. He described the Preface as a 'cowardly and disgraceful attack by a writer who has abused the privilege of anonymity which was accorded to him'. It was Taylor who supported the Synod's Broadcasting Officer, John Barton, in his refusal even to release the text of the Preface to the broadcasting and television newsrooms, an act of partisan censorship which was never rebuked.

The next to join the fray was Bishop Bill Westwood of Peterborough. In an excellent study of the *Crockford's* affair, William Oddie comments on Westwood:

In his answers, he adopted a tactic to be followed widely over the succeeding days: to ignore or sidestep the substantial criticisms of the preface, concentrating on the allegedly underhand nature of the attack, the contemptible character of the attacker, and the impropriety of such criticism emanating from the heart of the Church bureaucracy itself.[7]

This mirrored the carefully prepared attack made to the Press Association, later on the same day by Dr Habgood, Archbishop of York, in which he described the Preface as 'scurrilous' and 'sour and vindictive', and its author as a 'disappointed cleric'. (Westwood was to use a similar phrase, 'disappointed clergyman'.)[8]

Steve Doughty, writing in the *Daily Mail*, reported:

The liberals say that the author is a disappointed academic passed over for promotion – which they say fits Dr Bennett and a number of others passed over by the Crown Appointments Commission which chooses bishops. This line attempts entirely to discredit the *Crockford's* piece on the grounds that it is the work of an embittered man . . . or woman.

There is a fundamental intolerance in ecclesiastical liberalism which belies its name, and no one is more adept at its exercise than those members of the House of Bishops who fall under Bennett's category of elitist liberal, and nowhere is their power more abused than when they substitute the practised sneer for the exercise of true leadership. It is a propensity at the heart of episcopacy which must be a major cause of the moral paralysis which afflicts bishops in their exercise of Christian leadership, exacerbated of course by the principle of collegiality but in the end far more serious in its results.

In the General Synod debate on the *Crockford's* affair, I tried to set out the process which follows when one tries to engage in debate on the major moral and spiritual issues of the day, and I quote it in full now, seven years later, with the very deepest regret that nothing has changed:

Anyone who has challenged the view of the liberal establishment is aware of the sequence of events which follows – and it has happened to me many times. First of all, the friends who gave support and encouragement suddenly are not there, and that is part of my guilt in relation to Garry's tragic death. One can readily understand why this happens. Then, when a reasoned argument is offered, instead of a reasoned response it produces vulgar abuse from those who ought to know better – and Garry had his share of that.

Because that goes unrebuked by our Church leaders [by which I meant the bishops], and seems sometimes to be encouraged by them, it is then taken up by the lesser fry, and to it they add distortion, often accusing us of stating the very views that we have specifically denied or denounced – and that has happened to me many times.

Worst of all, as with Soviet dissidents, we come to expect the suggestion of mental instability: we cannot be against women priests for theological reasons, the integrity of which must be acknowledged, but because we feel threatened by women or have sexual hang-ups.

I dismissed as bizarre the situation made to me after Garry's death that people would now say he was unbalanced. But it happened and, frankly, it was at this point that I felt soiled and ashamed to be a member of such a Church.[9]

I said that in the pain of the aftermath of the *Crockford's* affair and in the grief and bereavement at the unnecessary death of a friend and colleague. I wish I could now say that I was mistaken, or at least that the leadership of our Church no longer behaved in such a manner. I have to say that I could repeat the speech without changing a single word, and that is a great sadness, given the much deeper crisis in which the Church of England, only a few years later, now finds itself. After Bennett's death, Dr Habgood mocked the media presentation of the dead author of the Preface as 'a misunderstood prophet who had dared to criticise an all-powerful establishment, been savaged by it, and died in despair at a Church which rejected him'.[10] But he was precisely that, and none of his friends could have written an epitaph which was more apt.

In the present crisis in which the Church of England is enmeshed, it has to be said that no one has worked harder than Dr Habgood in attempting to make it possible for those holding the two totally incompatible views on the ordination of women to remain together within the Church. His leadership in this process has staved off, even if only temporarily, a crisis much greater than the one which presently exists.

The Act of Synod, which established the appointment of Provincial Episcopal Visitors (the so-called 'flying bishops') to minister to those unable to accept episcopal care from bishops who have ordained women, has provided a breathing space for those hurt and bereaved by the Synod's action in approving the ordination of women. It remains to be seen whether that 'breathing space' will prove to be no more than a compassionate terminal care, or whether it will represent a means for a long-term future within the Church of England for those repeatedly branded as heretics by Archbishop George Carey.

But it proved to be one positive result of the concept of collegiality, where a powerful and much-respected leader – Dr John Habgood – persuaded the House of Bishops, in the case of some members very much against their will, to act together for the good of the whole Church. How committed the bishops as a whole are to the Act and to the principle that two integrities now exist side by side in the Church, both to be respected, one can only guess.

Certainly some bishops are behaving badly to those clergy who refuse to toe the line, and the 'flying bishops' are finding that they must raise more of such issues with the two archbishops than they would really wish. But they are tough men, firm in their faith and ready to speak out, quite unlike their fellow bishops.

They will not endure endless committees, nor be expected to perform the 'establishment' functions of other bishops. They will preach the faith, pastor their clergy, spending endless hours in travel in the process. In other words, we may quite inadvertently be seeing the restoration of episcopacy in its New Testament pattern, eventually providing a spiritual leadership in the nation which is impossible to the present bench.

11

Leadership in the Nation

O momentary grace of mortal man,
Which we more hunt for than the grace of God!
Richard III, iii.iv.95

The General Synod motion on homosexuality, as amended
by the Bishop of Chester's proposals, ended with these
words: 'that all Christians are called to be exemplary in
all spheres of morality, including sexual morality, and
that holiness of life is particularly required of Christian
leaders'.[1]

In the debate, Bishop Baughan explained why he
supported the need for holiness in Christian leaders. 'I
suggest that it is the New Testament way to lift up that
standard of holiness and to call for personal response,
even avoiding behaviour that we may think acceptable
if it would cause someone else to stumble.'[2] But he
carefully rejected the demand in the original motion
by Tony Higton, that 'all Christian leaders are called to
be exemplary in all spheres of morality, including sexual
morality, as a condition of being appointed or remaining
in office,' pointing out, rightly, that all have fallen short
of the perfection which God requires and ought to resign
immediately if the motion were passed.

The moral standards required of Christian leaders are
nonetheless high, and 'holiness of life' is certainly expected

of them. Sometimes they fall short of God's ideal, and one is reminded of the guiding principle of Chaucer's Poor Parson:

> If gold ruste, what shal iren do?
> For if a preest be foul, on whom we truste,
> No wonder is a lewed man to ruste;
> And shame it is, if a preest take keep,
> A shiten shepherde and a clene shepe.[3]

As we have already seen, this is clearly not a view shared by some of the bishops of the Church of England, and one of the most frequent criticisms in the letters I received after the Prince Charles affair was that I was commenting on the behaviour of the Prince of Wales when some bishops did nothing about the immorality of a small minority of their clergy. It was not a criticism I could easily deny. Not unlike the advice of a certain bishop to Prince Charles ('do a bit of shooting'), another urged a priest who had left his wife for a much younger woman, an unmarried mother, 'Get a divorce, keep your head down for eighteen months, and we'll be able to find you another parish.'

There was in that case no suggestion of repentance but, even allowing for the proper Christian charity which must be showed to a sinner who turns away from his former life, most people would feel something was amiss where, in Chaucer's words, there was a 'shiten sheperde and a clene shepe'. Indeed, the canon law of the Church of England requires a certain standard of behaviour from its ministers:

> A minister shall not give himself to such occupations, habits, or recreations as do not befit his sacred calling, or may be detrimental to the performance of the duties of his office, or tend to be a just cause of offence to others; and at all times he shall be diligent to frame

and fashion his life and that of his family according to the doctrine of Christ, and to make himself and them, as much as in him lies, wholesome examples and patterns to the flock of Christ.[4]

Any suggestion that the Church is only concerned with the sins of the flesh, that it has, in the words of the Bishop of Truro, Michael Ball, 'hang-ups about certain aspects of morality', are dispelled by the wide-ranging nature of that definitive piece of canon law, which is binding upon all the clergy. It does not of course mean that all (or even any) will expect to be perfect, never falling from grace, never committing the smallest sin. But it does mean that the expectation is that they will fashion their lives in every respect in accordance with God's law and seek his forgiveness and grace in their failures. And moreover, the canon makes clear that these are the requirements of his office as a minister of God.

But does this extend to other Christians not in the sacred ministry? Or even to other citizens living by a code of decency towards those who are their neighbours? And if it applies to leadership within the Church, can it also be expected to apply to leadership in society? Do those who lead need to display exemplary conduct in their private as well as their public lives?

The Times and the Archbishop of York thought not, at least so far as the Prince of Wales was concerned. I had asked the question (no more): if his attitude to his vows of matrimony was so cavalier, has he the right to be trusted in this second solemnity? (That is, in taking the coronation vows, also in church and before God.) I went on:

The answer of course may be that the nation would trust him to do this, that attitudes to morality – and to matrimony – have so changed that the idea of fidelity is outdated.[5]

The Times editorial thundered against this 'so-called "moral argument"', but apparently only so far as an heir to the throne was concerned. It went on to suggest that I had confused the respective public roles of king and politician:

> An MP found to be unfaithful to his wife is guilty of hypocrisy if he has campaigned for family values; in a more general sense, it may also be argued that his deceit makes him unworthy of the public's trust. Rarely can a politician's life be wholly held distinct from his private conduct.[6]

The Archbishop of York too, having first supported *The Times* editorial in its refutal of my 'fallacious' argument about Charles and his marriage vows, agreed that

> it is not so easy to dispose of the general suspicion that flaws in private life may have their reflection in public life. Recurrent scandals about the private lives of politicians reveal that answers to questions about the relation between public and private morality are not simple.[7]

Writing a little later for the York Diocesan newspaper, *SeeN* (January 1994), Archbishop Habgood returned to this theme, supporting my own frequent assertion that the point about adultery is not what happens between the sheets but that it is a breakage of trust:

> The truest motive for refraining from adultery is that by undermining fidelity and trust it destroys a precious human quality. In Christian thought one of the key characteristics of God is summed up in a word variously translated as steadfastness, faithfulness or mercy. Here

is the rock on which the life of faith is built, and it is against the background of this belief that the possibilities of reflecting such steadfastness in our relation with another human being are to be grasped.[8]

There is surely nothing (to use the words of *The Times* leader) 'mischievous, fallacious, aggressive in language and wholly regrettable' in asking if a politician who shows by having both wife and mistress that he lacks fidelity may not also be deficient in the steadfastness necessary for political leadership.

When the then Defence Minister John Profumo was found to be sharing a call-girl with a Soviet diplomat, questions were raised about national security. Archbishop Habgood in his article in *The Times* suggested that 'efforts to bolster disapproval by linking sexual adventures with security risks may frequently turn out to be rationalisations'.[9]

But it is precisely because such sexual adventures usually involve breakage of that fidelity and trust, which as Dr Habgood has elsewhere pointed out indicates the absence of qualities of steadfastness and faithfulness, that questions are naturally raised about fidelity in another area of an adventurer's activities. And because Profumo had to admit that he had deceived the House of Commons – another breakage of fidelity and trust – he was forced to resign.

For a government minister to have lied to the House of Commons is usually (or at least used to be) sufficient for his resignation to be offered and accepted. It is clear why this should be so: if he has lied on one issue, can members ever be sure that he is not lying in other statements which he may make to the House? It may be wholly unjust that he should henceforth be suspect if in the heat of the parliamentary moment he had once deliberately misled his colleagues. But the procedures of a body like Parliament depend on certain proprieties of this nature in order properly to conduct business.

But so do ordinary day-to-day social relationships: a society cannot survive if no one who is part of it is to be trusted, no more than can a family or a friendship survive if mutual trust is for ever under threat or question. To return to the matter of formal logic, if I can make the statement, 'Everything Jack says is the truth', then any statement which Jack makes to me I can deduce to be the truth. But if on one occasion Jack lied to me, while I cannot assume that everything he tells me is a lie (which in logical terms would involve the logical fallacy of assuming the general from the particular), I cannot either make the statement, 'Jack has said this, and everything Jack says is the truth, so this must be true.'

If we are to carry on satisfactorily the ordinary business of living within a family or a society, then we need to be sure that the strong do not dominate the weak, that there is fidelity in relationships, that we do not lie to or steal from each other, that life is sufficiently respected that we do not risk injury or death from those around us. There may in fiction be some honour among thieves, but a family of thieves would be foolish to place absolute trust in any of its members.

But what is true of every person in society must also be true of our leaders. We are right to expect a basic public morality from our political leaders, not because they are in positions which require higher standards than apply to everyone else but rather because those standards apply to all, rich and poor, leaders and led, if society is to survive. Moreover, we are right to demand that the private and public morality of the politician or other leader are equally acceptable, not simply for the avoidance of hypocrisy but because the one affects the other.

Tony Blair, in a speech just before the beginning of his campaign for the leadership of the British Labour Party, pointed out that 'the values of a decent society are, in many ways, the values of the family unit'. It was unfortunate for John Major's government that it faced in 1993 a run of misfortune as scandals emerged about the private lives of some of its members. David Mellor and Tim Yeo were eventually forced to resign after revelations about the conduct of their private lives, but not before the Prime Minister had made valiant but vain attempts to save their careers.

But a party which claims to be the guardian of family life, an upholder of family values, and a supporter of a 'back-to-basics' campaign, cannot close its eyes to activities of its leaders which undermine those very principles. It may be hard, but the public prefer not to accept double standards from those whom they have elected to lead them. Moreover, it does seem that a party which has been in power for many years begins to believe in its own absolute right to behave as it wishes.

Writing in 1887 to the author of an historical article with which he had disagreed, Lord Acton complains that the author has said 'that people in authority are not to be snubbed or sneered at from our pinnacle of moral rectitude'.

I cannot accept your canon that we are to judge Pope and King unlike other men, with a favoured presumption that they did no wrong. If there is any presumption, it is the other way, against holders of power, increasing as the power increases . . . *Power tends to corrupt, and absolute power corrupts absolutely* [emphasis added]. Great men are almost always bad men, even when they exercise influence and not authority: still more when you superadd the tendency or the certainty of corruption by authority . . . The inflexible integrity of the moral code is to me the secret of the authority, the dignity, and the utility of history. If we debase the currency for the sake of genius or success or reputation, we may debase it for the sake of a man's influence, of his religion, of his party, of the good cause which prospers by his credit and suffers by his disgrace.[10]

There is a certain sense of *déjà vu* in the fact that it was to a leading churchman of the day, Bishop Mandell Creighton of London, that Lord Acton felt it necessary to write this rebuke and warning. It is hard to agree with the blanket statement that 'great men are nearly always bad men', but the dictum that 'power tends to corrupt and absolute power corrupts absolutely' should be taken to heart by all who exercise any kind of authority or leadership function, in Church or in State.

There is however a major difference between the qualities required for leadership in the Church and those required for political leadership. We have already noted three factors which influence bishops and which are almost uniformly damaging to their exercise of effective leadership.

The first is the overwhelming need to hold the right views, make the right speeches, be noted by the right people, if preferment is to come, which qualities in a churchman – who is in any case supposed to reject any concept of a career structure in the service of Jesus Christ – must almost inevitably undermine his integrity. It is a cruel but familiar joke that at a new bishop's consecration, when his fellow-bishops gather in a kind of rugby scrum around him at the moment of his consecration, they are not invoking the Holy Spirit but removing his backbone.

But a politician, if he is to be a useful member of the government, must first shine on the back-benches, display his expertise in this or that field, and generally present himself as someone who could eventually become a member of the Cabinet. It was as followers of a master whose purpose was to be as a servant that the apostles James and John were rebuked for seeking the best seats in the new kingdom, and not as modern politicians aspiring to serve the nation through the particular manifesto of their party.

The second inhibiting factor in the exercise of episcopal leadership is the concept of collegiality which has developed over the years, by which public disagreement is avoided and bishops show a more or less united front, in such leadership as they exhibit. In a political party on the other hand, there must be a collective responsibility at least among the Cabinet or Shadow Cabinet to hold firm to the party manifesto. Such back-benchers who do not aspire to higher office can perform a useful task in pointing to new principles or in calling for a return to former principles now abandoned, but it is right for politicians to seek a collegiality in cabinet if policies are to be put into practice. Indeed in government or opposition, business could not be done effectively if pragmatism did not sometimes override absolute principle. And there are always the voices of such members as Dennis Skinner to remind members that in the end they exist for the principles and not for the pragmatism.

The third factor, allied to the second, is the issuing of a party line from the press office which bishops are encouraged to follow, either by the authority of its source or by peer-pressure from fellow-bishops. A wanderer from the fold would hesitate to face the spoken or unspoken disapproval of his fellows at the next bishops' meeting. But in a modern democracy, with a highly sophisticated media system and presence, it is essential that a professionally directed press office should be ready at all times to guide party spokesmen in the best presentation of manifesto policy.

Moral issues of the sort where bishops could, but on the whole do not, give a lead are rarely clear-cut, and it does no harm for this to be expressed in episcopal comments with less than a common mind. A recent example of this, which is also the fine expression on the role which spiritual leaders can play within the secular state, came in a debate in the House of Lords on the proposal to lower the age of consent for homosexual behaviour.[11]

The Roman Catholic peer, the Duke of Norfolk, spoke to his own amendment to retain the age of consent at twenty-one while he suggested 'a longer chance for young men to work out their sexual orientation when they grow up'.

Another Roman Catholic, Lord Longford, supported him, suggesting that reducing the age of consent would increase the corruption of young boys by middle-aged and elderly men, while the former Chief Rabbi, Lord Jakobovits, hesitated even at a minimum of twenty-one on the grounds that acts which were seen as immoral did not suddenly become moral when someone came of age. The amendment was also supported by the Bishop of Chester, who spoke up as one of the Lords Spiritual.

But the Archbishop of York argued for the lowering of the age of consent to eighteen rather than sixteen, since to have a small age difference said something about 'society's acceptance of heterosexuality as the norm'. He pointed out that in the past 'some appalling things have been done to homosexuals in the name of God. I would not wish to endorse the hatred and contempt in which many of them have been held.'[12]

The expression of divergence of views between different religious leaders was an aid rather than a hindrance to debate, and enhanced the contributions which they made.

Of course, the bishops too have their party manifesto in scriptures and creeds, and if their adherence to the principle of collegiality were allied to an unswerving acceptance and presentation of the doctrines which by their office they are commissioned to guard, then collegiality would be as justifiable as it is in the political sphere.

It is a major factor in the crisis now affecting the Church of England that this is not so, that instead of banishing erroneous and strange doctrines, some bishops have embraced them with a fervour that will deceive the very elect. Whereas in the political sphere, Cabinet responsibility would quickly rally to distance the party from heresy, in the Church the silence it induces effectively endorses and strengthens the false teaching.

Moreover whereas Christian leadership, like the Christian life, must be centred on the doctrine that we are saved through faith and not through works, for the politician survival comes not through adherence to party principle but by the practicality of those principles evidenced in how they are seen to work.

The corruption of power arises through its enjoyment, and it is this which increases as power increases. Nonetheless, I do believe that in our British system of democratic parliamentary government, few people enter politics for any other reason than service, in the belief that the principles of the party they have chosen to represent are the best for the good health and wealth of the greatest number of people. That is true at least as much of those who seek ordination, and though both church and state will have a share of rogues and vagabonds, or, more likely, of temporisers and compromisers, that is no more than a recognition that both Church and State consist not of saints but of sinners.

When the truth is recognised that all, leaders and led, are sinners, or in other words that all fall short of the best that is possible for the human condition, the danger arises that the best will be regarded not merely as unattainable but as irrelevant. The good health of society does not only demand that politician, parson or prince live by the rules and values which make for a good community: the rules and values are those to which every citizen must aspire if society is to survive in any form that is worthwhile.

12

The Epilogue – What Next?

Great griefs I see, medicine the less.
Cymbeline, IV.ii.243

Twenty years have passed by: it is the year 2015 and Queen Elizabeth II is in her ninetieth year. Her eldest son and heir to the throne, Charles, increasingly arthritic from the many sporting injuries of his younger days, now seems unlikely to succeed, and rumours abound that he will soon abdicate the heirdom in favour of William, the eldest son of his first marriage to Lady Diana Spencer.

Lord Blair, formerly Sir Anthony Blair and the longest-serving Prime Minister in living memory, was elected by the House of Commons to the newly constituted Upper House, the first former minister to enter the Lords after the radical and much-disputed reform which occupied so much parliamentary time in the last Labour administration.

All governments eventually run out of ideas, and the need for a change sends popularity levels in the polls soaring to new heights or sinking to unprecedented depths. It was in the end not surprising that the country decided a radical change was necessary, as a result of which so many familiar faces disappeared from the parliamentary scene after the election two years ago.

The streets of Britain are now safer to walk and the

danger of mugging, rape, violent attack and the many serious anxieties of 1995 are a distant memory. With twenty years of growing emphasis on human responsibility as the corollary of human rights, moral standards have improved beyond measure, though there is (and there will always be) still far to go. With the family-life legislation of the Blair government, much criticised and resisted by liberal Church leaders of the day, the lot of young and old alike has improved, not least in the deprived areas of our cities.

So much water has passed under the political bridge in the last ten years that it is hard to realise at the turn of the century, the dogmas of political correctness had taken such hold on the nation's life that for a short but chaotic period, quotas were required in so many areas of life – in business and employment, on committees, in parliamentary membership . The need was demanded to achieve exact proportions in the membership and representation on all bodies of young, middle-aged and old, male and female, homosexual, heterosexual and bi-sexual, male and female, Afro-Caribbean, Caucasian (with special subdivisions where appropriate for English, Scots, Welsh, Irish and European), Asian (with sub-divisions of Indian, Pakistani, Oriental and 'other') and all the rest in attacks on attitudes of racism, sexism, ageism, fat-ism, classism and other now-discredited categories.

When the devastating London School of Economics report on the so-called Political Correctness Act proved that government and commerce, not to mention the educational world, were breaking down through the total impossibility of promoting the best people or appointing those with the expertise necessary for any committee or organisation, the initial refusal to act on its findings caused widespread demonstrations (remember the taunting chants: 'PC-LSE: PC-LSE'?).

It was only the rearguard action by the Official Church

of England's Secretary for Social Affairs, with the support of the General Synodical Council, which delayed its repeal. Her many appeals to the European Commission on Human Rights meant that every clause of the Political Correctness (Reform) Act was scrutinised in the minutest detail at enormous cost both to the taxpayer and to the impoverished Official Church of England, the only area of national life where political correctness still reigns supreme.

As we all know it was an expense which finally caused the Official Church of England to call in the Official Receiver, though the Archbishop of Canterbury, the Most Revd Cissy H. Shearmend, quickly appeared on television to reassure her flock that this was only an interim measure which did not indicate that her Church was unable to pay its way. Bankrupt it may not be, but it is changed beyond all recognition from the Church which some will remember of 1995.

The ordination of the first women to the priesthood in 1994 caused a greater sea-change in the Church than anyone could have predicted. Over the next five years, about 500 eligible male clergy took the compensation offered by the Ordination of Women (Financial Provisions) Measure, until the General Synod closed this loop-hole by its infamous Financial Provisions (Amendment) Measure. By the terms of this Measure, the compensatory provisions were removed, and in addition all serving clergy were required to attend a Renewal of Priestly Vows ceremony every Maundy Thursday, at which they were directed to make the amended Declaration of Assent, a strict oath of obedience to the bishop, and a declaration under Canon A4 that they recognise without qualification that

Those who are made, ordained, or consecrated bishops, priests, or deacons, according to the Ordinal, are lawfully made, ordained, or consecrated, and are

accounted by me to be truly bishops, priests, or deacons.

The Synod's attempt to extend this to clergy pensioners,
as a condition of continuing to receive a pension, was
eventually abandoned only after the threat of court action,
and at the intervention of Sir Frank Field in the last year of
his long parliamentary career. It was a foolhardy proposal
and its injustice – widely compared to the Maxwell
affair when thousands of Maxwell Group pensioners were
defrauded – caused widespread defections from the ailing
Church of England and was one of the catalysts which led
to the establishment of the so-called 'orthodox' Anglican
Church.

The two Provincial Episcopal Visitors appointed under
the 1994 Act of Synod to care for clergy and lay people
unable to accept the ordination of women, were quickly
joined by a third, as it became clear that their nickname of
'flying bishop' in fact indicated the reality of this ministry.
They were responsible for vast areas and each covered up
to 80,000 miles by car each year, ministering to those who
called for this service. The treatment of clergy in their care
by the established bishops was not good, and it was necessary each month for them to refer cases of persecution or
mistreatment to the appropriate archbishop, though these
had little power of redress, other than exhortation.

It was the General Synod elected in 1995 that marked
the beginning of change. Traditional catholics and classical
evangelicals who had played a major part in the opposition
to women priests had either resigned their orders or their
membership of the Church of England, or refused to
stand for election, or if they stood were not elected,
so that the rough division of the Synod into one third
traditionalists (catholic or evangelical), one third liberal
catholic and one third reformed evangelical, which had
marked its life in its first twenty-five years of existence,
no longer held.

The traditionalists were reduced to a small and ineffective rump, unable to influence synodical proposals, too weak to gain election to boards and councils, so that their contribution was almost totally neutralised. But only 'almost'; for it remained vitally important for one group, however small, to remind the Church's central policy-forming body that, however much such influences were now despised or marginalised, scripture and tradition still remained the bedrock of Anglicanism, at least in its official formularies. Unfortunately, it did not prevent a remorseless advance of liberal ideas becoming part of the life of the Church of England, without regard to the effect on its ordinary, grass-roots membership.

As early as July 1994, preliminary ideas were put to the General Synod on the use of feminist language for God, to be incorporated in a future revision of liturgy and ready for the publication of a revised Alternative Service Book. Cautiously, the technique which was proposed closely followed that which had proved so successful in the Episcopal Church of the United States. Assurances were given that initially God would not be called 'she', and there was recognition that some would feel this was contrary to scriptural evidence. But the cultural conditioning of Jesus was emphasised and tentative moves in the direction of avoiding masculine references to God were encouraged, as well as 'uncontroversial' similes in which Jesus was compared to a mother looking after her children.

It was an unnecessary caution, for the Synod which replaced it in 1995 soon found it had the muscle to introduce changes in liturgy, ethics and doctrine without fear of a long rearguard action from traditionalists. The Prayer Book of 2000, which coincided with legislation outlawing all other liturgies, especially the Book of Common Prayer of 1662, expunged all references to God as 'he', and avoided descriptions of God as lord, king, almighty, and suchlike as imperialistic and consequently inappropriate to the culture and spirit of the age.

By the year 2000, a vast legislative programme had been completed, largely without serious reference to the wider membership of the Church of England, save to those activists prepared to sit on deanery and diocesan bodies. The Convocation regulations forbidding the marriage in church of anyone with a former partner still alive had been rescinded, and the safeguards restricting such remarriage to certain categories were quickly abandoned in favour of a free-for-all.

One result was that it enabled the heir to the throne to be married by the Archbishop of Canterbury in a ceremony in Westminster Abbey, even though both partners had been divorced. The *Church Times*, in one of its last issues, hailed it as a great day for the Church and a great day for the nation. 'It marks the final watershed between the old reactionary days when the Church allowed itself to be bound by rules outdated by two millennia and the dawning of the New Age of freedom. We have now redeemed the secular from the inhibitions of medieval religious taboos.'

The debate on the conflict between the woman's right to choose and the unborn infant's right to life succumbed to feminist pressure in favour of abortion on demand; while in the same way, the strength of the pro-gay lobby in the 1995 intake on to the General Synod assured the passing of motions supporting the rights of practising homosexual men and women not only to be ordained but also to have permanent relationships blessed in a form of 'marriage'.

The parson's freehold was abolished on the grounds that the clergy should be subject to dismissal in the same manner as that suffered by most other professions, though without regard to the vocational aspects of clerical life in lower salaries and tied accommodation. It was applied retrospectively and as a result many clergy – male and female – who criticised secularising trends in the Church were subject to dismissal, for it removed that essential safeguard the clergy had enjoyed to preach the gospel as they saw it without fear, and regardless of episcopal pressure or even episcopal heresy. Television pictures of grieving clergy families turned out on to the street by bailiffs, for no real reason other than their continued adherence to the faith and practice which their Church had once upheld, caused much criticism and many defections from the Church of England.

The supply of new ordinands diminished, so that with retirements, resignations, redundancies and forced dismissals on doctrinal grounds, the numbers in full-time ministry dropped by almost 50 per cent in ten years. With the collapse of the parochial system and the abandonment of the concept that a vicar or rector of the Church of England was to minister to the whole population, congregations declined rapidly, and with it the income they had provided. In the year 2005, an archbishop's commission was set up to meet the crisis, but its recommendations were too little and too late.

In the early days of Provincial Episcopal Visitors, it became apparent that the 'flying bishops' were a new breed of episcopal leader. Although they had been chosen as men likely to 'fit in', that is to be ready to accommodate to the wishes of the more senior diocesan bishops, it was soon found, as with Henry II and Thomas à Becket, that two different ideologies clashed face to face in an uncompromising absolutism.

The 'flying bishops' were men who had never been ready to compromise for the sake either of approval or of preferment, and taking the purple brought no change in that. They preached a faith based firmly in Holy Scripture, unamended by the pressures of secularism, and were totally committed to the fundamentals of Anglicanism. In the dying years of the twentieth century, it was as inevitable that they would be in head-on conflict with the ecclesiastical establishment as it was that Becket should be in conflict with the Crown.

As each new change in doctrine or ethical standards was

introduced by the General Synod, the three bishops said, in effect, 'It doesn't happen in our part of the Church of England. If you don't like it, here is a list of parishes with priests who remain faithful.' Gradually, members of congregations voted with their feet and transferred their allegiance to parish churches which suited their beliefs. It was not of course all one-way traffic; but for every person who transferred to a 'liberal' parish, six or eight moved in the opposite direction.

As the opposition to this grew within the Official Church of England so action against those in the flying bishops' jurisdiction increased; and as it did, so the contributions which persecuted parishes were expected to give to the central work of the Church diminished to the point that it could not be sustained. In a matter of a few years into the new century, staff numbers at Church House, Westminster, the central headquarters, had been reduced from just under 200 at the height of its powers to a rump of about 25 people, administrators, board secretaries and assistants.

Meanwhile the Forward in Faith organisation, originally established to give care and counsel to those hurt by the decision to ordain women, became rich and influential, as contributions and affiliation fees poured in from the disaffected faithful. Gradually it began to give a spiritual leadership to church and nation which gave no ground to secular pressures, and by 2005 it had become one of the most respected bodies in national affairs.

It was perhaps inevitable that a division should take place in the Church of England, and with the benefit of hindsight it is surprising that it took place only in 2012. The refusal of the establishment to appoint bishops to replace the three original Provincial Episcopal Visitors led to the bishops taking the law into their own hands, in the 'illegal' consecrations of 2003, and the deliberate and necessary expansion of their numbers from three to twelve. It was pointed out then that the usual Sunday attendance in parishes with a Forward in Faith priest gave a national total higher than in the far greater number of churches in the care of the forty-four diocesan and sixty-four suffragan bishops.

As the bishops began also to ordain clergy to serve in their own self-sufficient parishes, problems with regard to pension rights for the newly ordained, ownership of houses and rights of occupation, meant an inexorable move to legal challenges. When an attempt was made to require annual vows to be taken which would have offended the consciences of orthodox clergy and with it restrictions on pension entitlement, it came as a relief that Parliament stepped in, not on theological grounds but simply to preserve religious freedom and to avoid injustice.

Based on the precedent of the Wee Frees in Scotland, Parliament passed the Church of England (Division of Assets) Act which gave the traditionalists a proportionate share in the assets and buildings of the Church of England, and effectively confirmed the schism which had been developing between the two warring parts of the Church.

The traditionalists took the name, The Anglican Church, to show its unity with traditionalist groups in other countries with whom links had developed over the years, as well as opening up the possibility of closer ties with the Roman Catholic and Orthodox churches and with groups of traditional believers in Lutheran and other protestant churches, with whom contacts had been maintained throughout the years of persecution and ridicule.

It has been a potent indication that though the truths of God may be abandoned by his own people, he does not abandon his Church – evidence once again in history that even the gates of hell shall not prevail against it. And for the nation the years of flaccid leadership from the Church of England are consigned to the past, now that the Anglican Church is fulfilling the task that its errant mother abandoned, bringing spiritual truths to bear on the nation's problems, on politicians' mistakes and blindnesses, and on the duties and responsibilities of every citizen, from the most humble to the highest in the land.

Notes

Unless indicated otherwise, the Bible quotations have been taken from the Revised Standard Version.

Chapter 1: Introduction

1 *Daily Mail*, 18 June 1994: Saturday Essay by Alan Massie

Chapter 2: One Day's Problems – and Another's

1 *Daily Telegraph*, 2 February 1994, article by Lesley Garner: 'Goodbye to Shame – and Hello! to Blighted Lives'
2 *Daily Telegraph*, 2 February 1994
3 *Daily Mail*, 2 February 1994
4 *The Times*, 2 February 1994
5 *Daily Mail*, 18 June 1994, article by Paul Johnson
6 1 Corinthians 5:11
7 Preface to Holy Communion Service, *Book of Common Prayer* (1662)
8 1 Corinthians 11:29

Chapter 3: Royal Affairs

1 Sir Maurice Powicke, *The Thirteenth Century* (OUP) p. 83
2 *The Times*, 8 December 1993

3 *The Times*, 11 December 1993
4 *SeeN* (York diocesan newspaper), January 1994
5 *The Times*, 11 December 1993
6 *Mail on Sunday*, 30 January 1994

Chapter 4: Christians in Glass Houses

1 John 8:3–11 (v.4, NJB)
2 Matthew 7:1–2
3 Mark 10:11–12
4 Matthew 5:32
5 Matthew 7:3–5
6 Matthew 5:27–28

Chapter 5: Faith, Grace and Truth

1 Luke 15:11–32 (author's own rendering)
2 Ephesians 1:6 (AV)
3 Ephesians 2:8
4 Luke 23:43
5 Matthew 9:6
6 Hugh Dawcs, *Freeing the Faith* (Triangle Books, SPCK) p. 45
7 Genesis 3 (NJB)

Chapter 6: A New Morality and a New God?

1 J. A. T. Robinson, *Honest to God* (SCM Prcss) p. 115
2 *Ibid.* p. 115
3 *Ibid.* p. 116
4 *Ibid.* p. 119
5 *Ibid.* p. 119
6 Matthew 5:18
7 Romans 7:18–19
8 Rodney Booth, *Winds of God* (WCC and Wood Lake Books Inc.) p. 11

9 Ephesians 2:8
10 The Burial of the Dead, *The Book of Common Prayer* (1662)
11 This report of my address (pp. 55–9) appeared in the *Church of England Newspaper*
12 Ephesians 3:17–19

Chapter 7: Politics and Pulpit

1 Edmund Burke, *Reflections on the Revolution in France* (1790)
2 *Ibid.*
3 Isaiah 1:4
4 Isaiah 1:15
5 Isaiah 1:16–17
6 Isaiah 58:6–7
7 Jeremiah 22:3
8 Jeremiah 34:9
9 Nehemiah 5:10–11
10 James 1:26–7
11 James 2:2–4
12 1 John 3:17–18
13 Luke 16:19–21
14 Matthew 25:41–46
15 Matthew 25:45
16 Matthew 23:23–24
17 John 15:18–19
18 James 4:4
19 Isaiah 1:17
20 1 Corinthians 12:31
21 General Synod, *Report of Proceedings*, vol. 9, no. 3, p. 1084
22 *Ibid.* p. 1085
23 *Ibid.* p. 1076
24 Report of the Anglican Pastoral Visit to Namibia, September 1989, p. 37
25 Lutheran World Federation press release, October 1989
26 General Synod Report, vol. 17, no. 2, p. 552

27 Karl Marx, *Critique of Hegel's Philosophy of Right*, Introduction (1843–4)
28 Charles Kingsley, *Letters to the Chartists* no. 2
29 Romans 12:2

Chapter 8: A Church Established

1 General Synod, *Report of Proceedings*, vol. 3, no. 4, p. 599
2 *Ibid.* p. 599
3 *Ibid.* p. 600
4 *Ibid.* p. 602
5 *Ibid.*
6 J. B. Black, *The Reign of Elizabeth* (OUP) p. 12
7 *Ibid.* p. 14
8 J. D. Mackie, *The Earlier Tudors* (OUP) p. 355
9 J. B. Black, p. 16
10 *Ibid.* p. 17
11 General Synod, *Report of Proceedings*, vol. 3, no. 4, p. 602
12 Matthew 23:6
13 1 Corinthians 12:31

Chapter 9: By Appointment Only

1 Oxford Dictionary of the Christian Church (OUP) *Congé d'élire* p. 329
2 J. R. H. Moorman, *History of the Church in England* (A & C Black) p. 279
3 *Ibid.* p. 281
4 Owen Chadwick, *The Victorian Church* (A & C Black) vol. 1, p. 121
5 *Ibid.* p. 476
6 Owen Chadwick, *Michael Ramsey* (OUP) p. 75
7 *Ibid.* p. 66
8 *Ibid.* p. 76
9 A. M. Ramsey, *Canterbury Pilgrim* (SPCK) p. 183
10 General Synod, *Report of Proceedings*, vol. 19, no. 1, p. 88
11 Moorman, p. 279
12 *Ibid.* p. 281

13 Edmund Burke, *Letters on a Regicide Peace, no. 3* (1797)
14 Acts of Apostles 1:26

Chapter 10: Leadership in the Church

1 General Synod, *Report of Proceedings*, vol. 18, no. 3,
  p. 913
2 *Ibid*. p. 946
3 *Ibid*. p. 932
4 *Ibid*.
5 General Synod Committee for Communications, *Annual
  Report 1993*, paragraph 15, p. 4
6 *Daily Mail*, 8 December 1993
7 William Oddie, *The Crockford's File* (Hamish Hamilton)
  p. 32
8 Press Association, *Nationwide* report, 3 December 1987
9 General Synod, *Report of Proceedings* (February 1988)
  vol. 19, no. 1, pp. 88–9
10 *Ibid*. p. 102

Chapter 11: Leadership in the Nation

1 General Synod, *Report of Proceedings*, vol. 18, no. 3,
  p. 956
2 *Ibid*. p. 932
3 Geoffrey Chaucer, *The Canterbury Tales*, Prologue
4 *Canons of the Church of England*, Canon C26, 'Of the
  Manner and Life of Ministers'
5 *The Times*, 8 December 1993
6 *Ibid*.
7 *The Times*, 11 December 1993
8 *SeeN* (York diocesan newspaper), January 1994
9 *The Times*, 11 December 1993
10 Sir J. E. E. Dalberg Acton, *Life and Letters of Mandell
  Creighton* (A & C Black) vol. 1, p. 370
11 Reported in the *Church of England Newspaper*
12 *The Times*, 21 June 1994